The R

By Michael Klein

Table of Contents

Foreword

Publius Scipio Africanus the Elder and Hannibal Barca were major players in the Second Punic War – known to Romans of the day as "Hannibal's War. However, neither the conflict or the family histories began with the Second Punic War. In fact, the Punic wars grew out of territorial disputes between the two leading powers of the day, the Phoenicians and the Romans. The Greeks, Egyptians and Syrians were also players in these events, but they were the supporting cast, so to speak, in these episodes.

Carthage, the great Phoenician city (the word "Punic" derives from the Roman word for Phoenician) was founded around 814 BC. Settlers from Tyre claimed the land, and constructed the sea port. The area was fertile, and many of the settlers farmed the land surrounding Carthage. Others continued to carry out the ocean voyaging and sea trade for which the Phoenicians were famous. It should also be noted here that the Phoenicians are the same people as the Biblical Canaanites.

Meanwhile, elsewhere in the world, the people who would become Romans were having their fair share of difficulties. There are a variety of stories about the founding of Rome, including the familiar story about Romulus and Remus, the twins were reared by wolves and who founded Rome on two hillsides. Archeologists and anthropologists are by no means in absolute agreement on the origins of the Roman people, but there are some stories that are fairly consistently mentioned.

One of these stories is that the Romans were actually Etruscans, and that the Etruscans came from Asia. One legend has it that in a certain kingdom, the people were starving. There was so little food that they drew lots, and people ate on alternate days. At last the situation became so bad, that this no long sufficed, so the

Etruscan king used the lots to divide his people into two groups: those who would remain with him, and those who would sail away with his son to find more hospitable lands.

The son, who was named Tyrrhennus, helped to found cities on the coast of the area that is now Italy. At first the Etruscans were mostly in scattered villages, but as time went on, they clustered together more closely, forming larger settlements. They were agrarian, and they herded sheep. But they also developed a reputation as pirates. Of course, "piracy" was one of those words that rival cultures threw around at random, right along with "immoral" and "indecent." The Greek city states were also developing alongside the Roman culture.

There is a high probability that there were already people living in Italy at the time that the Etruscans landed and began founding their settlements. Mention is made of other tribal inhabitants who might very well have been there before the Etruscans. In all probability, they intermarried and the cultures blended.

The village of Rome was founded around 753 BC. For several hundred years there was no conflict between Rome and Carthage. In fact, they made several treaties and did a bustling bit of trade. (We won't mention piracy here – but there was probably some of that going on, as well.)

The Romans developed a society that had distinct social classes. At the top of the society were the Patricians, the founders who were the primary governing body. There was also a class called the Clients who were free, but took no part in the government. They were usually attached to one of the Patricians, or a Patron. At the bottom of the pecking order were the slaves, who had minimal rights (none) other than if they could come up with their purchase price they could buy their freedom. Also layered into this many textured society were the trades people – free men who were not clients or patrons, who ran small shops or created items that were beautiful or necessary. They might also take care of certain jobs that required more decision making than could be expected of a slave. Although, many masters took the long view, and put effort and expense into educating slaves for a variety of positions, including keeping accounts, writing, and fulfilling certain positions of responsibility.

To add to this mosaic of inhabitants, there were also resident foreigners, people who had come to Rome for trade or for other reasons. And there was the multitude of general residents, often referred to as plebian. After a time, a governing body called the Assembly provided representation for the plebeians – some of whom had become quite wealthy.

Each year two consuls were elected to run the city. In times of emergency, they might appoint a dictator, whose term in office was only six months. Perhaps such a person governed Rome while the consuls were in the field with the military.

Two quaestores were appointed each year to manage finances, under direction of the senate. Aediles were elected by the plebians in a section or quarter of the city and fulfilled a position roughly analogous to a policeman.

At first, many of the regulations of Rome were dictated from the top down by the Patrician, but as the centuries slid buy, the plebians gained more power and the ability to be voted into almost any office – including that of Dictator.

The problems with the neighbors did not arise in noticeable form until around 265 BC, when Rome had finished conquering the Roman peninsula.

Meanwhile, Carthage had also been growing in power and influence. Its territory had grown to include the island of Sicily. It was said that the lights of the cities of Sicily could be seen from the cities that were on the banks of the Italian peninsula.

The problem switched into high gear when one of the cities on Sicily appealed to Rome for help. Of course, that was music to the ears of the Roman senate – they were being invited to a conflict and they were more than happy to oblige. The only problem was that, even though the Etruscans had sailed to Rome, the current Romans were primarily land dwellers and farmers. In order to get their armies across to Sicily, they needed ships. At first they hired vessels to carry their armies across, but that proved to be less than satisfactory. The hired ships were not particularly interested in being drawn into a conflict with the Carthaginians, who were developing a growing reputation as able seamen. The Romans could fight on land, but that proved to be less than satisfactory when it came to taking over Sicily because the Carthaginians just kept landing shiploads of men and supplies from the seaward side.

Eventually the Romans did what they did best: they captured a Phoenician ship and copied it. The full story of how that all turned out is told in the second chapter of this book as a fireside tale.

In an imaginary setting, we look in on a world that might have been: Publius Cornelius telling his two young sons the story of how their Grandfather Gnaeus was captured by the Carthaginians, but was also instrumental in allowing the newly constructed Roman fleet to unload men and supplies in Sicily with scarcely a scratch.

That was the beginning of the First Punic War, and it belonged to the era of Publius Scipio Africanus' grandfather. Although Grandfather Gnaeus (not to be confused with Uncle Gnaeus) was censured for his error in judgement, he was again elected consul six years later. Nor was he the first of the Cornelius family to serve Rome. They had a distinguished record as upright Roman citizens and staunch supporters of the empire.

Indeed, the Cornelius family was one of the First Families of Rome. They knew their duty to city and country, and they willingly did it. In exchange, they expected honor, respect and – yes, indeed – a relative degree of wealth.

These were all to be had in Rome, in those days. These were the heyday of Rome's expansion. They built roads – wonderful roads. Indeed, there are Roman roads that still exist today. They conquered, and they incorporated the conquered into their society.

At the same time, the Carthaginians were trading, conquering and making their presence known. The two scruffy little nations had become big, grown-up political entities that were flexing their muscles and pushing hard against each other.

Our story begins with the Second Punic War. In fact, you could almost say that the story of the Punic Wars is the story of the family of Publius Scipio Cornelius Africanus. Not only did his grandfather, his father and his uncle – as well as himself – serve in the battles between Rome and Carthage, but so did his adopted grandson, Scipio Cornelius Africanus the Younger.

Finding the truth about Publius Scipio Cornelius Africanus is a challenge. Not only is there the difficulty of lost records – always a problem when trying to trace information that is more than two centuries old – but there is also the custom of telling outrageous stories for their intimidating effect on the other side.

Among the other things that Publius claimed, there was the story of how he was born by being cut from his mother's womb, and the enormous whopper he told of how his father was not the late Publius Cornelius who was cut down by enemies in Spain, but that daddy was really Poseidon, the powerful god of the sea. Apparently, he was completely indifferent to the light in which this cast his mother – women were not greatly considered at that time.

Publius Scipio Africanus and his brother Lucius Scipio took part in the Macedonian wars, as well. These involved Macedonia's having waited until it felt that Rome was worn down by its conflict with Carthage before starting to make aggressive moves toward Greece. Greece was far too close to Rome to ignore Phillip the Fifth quiet snabbling up of small Grecian villages.

The Macedonian War was not a popular one in Rome, and it was the beginning of the downfall of the brothers Scipio. But enough of that. Perhaps it is time to plunge into our story. As much as is possible, this book follows established cannon where Publius Scipio and the events that governed his adult life. But there are many areas where so little is known, that the author has relied upon snippets of information from a variety of sources to create plausible scenarios. These are inserted as background and for the amusement of the reader. They are plainly labeled, but it is the writer's hope that readers will enjoy these departures from strict historical fact. Perhaps one day you, the reader, will try your hand at writing a story or two about shadowy historical figures.

Certainly, Publius Scipio was not above embroidering upon the truth, so we are in good historical company when it comes to the weaving of tall tales.

Moreover, could it just be possible that in trying to slip into those historical shoes that we can begin to understand the continued struggle that seems to be woven around this fertile area, the lands around the Mediterranean Sea. It almost seems as if this area where three continents meet, where the spice trade, the silk trade and now oil exacerbate the struggle to survive, is almost like the umbilical of the world. Oh, to be sure there are other areas that are rich with resources, but it is possible that there are few places in the world that are so exceptionally rich in tradition or that have hosted so much interaction between cultures.

Perhaps if we reach back in time, if we try to understand the emotions, the drives and the circumstances that powered the conflicts between Rome and Carthage, and between Rome and Macedonia, we can begin to understand the workings of our modern world. Publius Scipio Africanus was but one man – but he was a man who stood tall amongst other historical giants, and whose actions were interwoven with major historical events of his time.

In the end, we find him -- but no, wait. That is getting ahead of our story. It is indeed time to focus on his tale. Indeed, you have no doubt, gentle reader, skipped over this foreword and headed on into the central theme of this narration.

Chapter 1: A Roman Childhood

Publius Cornelius Scipio, born around 236 BC, was the son of Consul Publius Scipio and Pomponi. Publius Scipio the elder was a patrician, and the third generation to serve as consul. Pomponi was the daughter of the plebian consul, Manius Pomponius Matho. Young Scipio was their first child, according to some accounts. According to others, he was the younger son. Although it would mean little to the Cornelii at the time, Hannibal Barca would have been about ten years old at the time of Scipio's birth. In the company of his father, Hamilcar (who would have been known to the household as a rival general), his brothers and brother-in-law, Hannibal was already in Spain as part of the Carthaginian efforts to take over that part of the country.

Not a lot is known about Scipio's childhood. Keeping records of the events surrounding children was not the fashion of the day, and although Scipio is said to have kept a diary it has long been lost. Gone also is Plutarch's account of his life. What remains are Livy's accounts of the man's military life, and mention of him in The Histories of Polybius plus various commentaries on his military prowess and his silver-tongued oratory.

Some accounts suggest that he was born by Caesarian, just as was the famous emperor, but this scarcely seems logical, since other accounts mention a younger brother, Lucius Cornelius Scipio Asiaticus. On the other hand, if Lucius was actually the eldest, this would pose no logistical problem. Since sources indicate that Publius and Lucius had the same mother, if Publius Scipio was the elder, the birth by surgery is somewhat problematical. Still, it is just possible that from somewhere there was an exceptionally skilled physician capable of preserving both mother and child in good health. Perhaps the boys were twins, and Scipio the elder by minutes instead of years. The past is full of Mystery – and evidence is scant.

Medical science was certainly in its infancy in those days. Surgical births were usually reserved as a last resort, when it was clear that the mother would not survive the birth. In truth, in such cases, it was rare for the baby to survive, either. With the scarcity of accounts, even the exact year of Scipio's birth is in question; the date is usually calculated from military accounts that record the year of the event and his age at the time of the event. With such a paucity of records, we are left to speculate what his life might have been like rather than to be able to say with certainty the kind of childhood that he might have had.

With mother and son or sons possibly in danger, Publius senior would probably have either engaged a wet nurse or have purchased a slave that had recently given birth so that young Publius would have a source of sustenance. Animal milk, at that time, was not always safe to drink; and as medical science has discovered, the best food for a human infant is human milk. Even if Pomponi was capable of nursing her own child, he would no doubt have gotten a serving woman for her, to help with the children and with needful personal care.

As soon as he could toddle, Publius would have begun learning how to behave as an adult. Although there was some recognition of childhood, for the most part children were treated like short adults. Since the family was patrician, they would probably have lived in a nice home in the city when Publius was serving his term in office; the rest of the time, they probably lived on their country estates, some distance outside of Rome.

It is likely that the family had slaves to work the farmland, and almost certain that Publius would have had a tutor who would have taken up looking after him as soon as he was old enough not to need his nurse – even though she might have continued to look after practical matters such as seeing to his clothing or making sure he washed his feet before going to bed.

Since the Cornelii were a military family, it is likely that Publius and Lucius began learning combat skills at an early age, as well as how to read, write and calculate. They would also have learned oration and possibly argumentation, since serving in the government would be expected of them. They would also have been encouraged to study famous battles, and would probably have played tabletop games of strategy.

Wealthy children did have toys, and it is probable that the boys had toy carts, perhaps a set of carved animals, and maybe even a set of carved toy soldiers. Toys of the day were made from wood, leather, and cloth scrap. Some of the little animals might have had wheels and a string by which they could be pulled. Dolls could be made with joints, and with costumes that could be put on and taken off. Perhaps the lads had one or two that could be dressed up as soldiers.

Even though Publius and Lucius would have been kept busy, it is probable that they found time to play. Even if toys were in short supply, sticks, stones and other naturally occurring objects could easily have been converted in a child's imagination into weapons, or made into small forts. The young of all sorts engage in play as part of their training for adulthood. We sometimes lose sight of that in our modern age; yet the toys that are provided for our children still reflect that principle.

Although we can only imagine what it might have been like in a Roman household, thanks to stories and legends we can gain some idea of what it might have been like to spend an ordinary day in a Roman household. Let's imagine a time when Publius was a gawky adolescent, just short of his twelfth year, and Lucius was a promising lad who would have been only a year or two younger. This is a process that is called "fictionalizing" and it used to be common in biographical works for elementary school children. So, turn back, pages of time and let us look in on the Cornellii on a morning when they were not going to war.

The hour was early, but Pomponi was already at her loom. She had finished spinning the season's wool the week before, and was determined to create a new tunic for Publius, Senior before the council season. Once that was done, she would use some of the remaining wool for herself. The boys would get tunics made from her husband's discarded tunics – suitably cut down to size. No point in wasting good fabric on youthful bodies that would heedlessly haul the fabric through muck and briar, giving the washer women cause to cluck their tongues and complain.

If there was enough wool, she might make Publius Scipio, Junior, a new tunic, however. He had been promised a trip to Rome with his father next council season. It was, quite clearly, time to begin thinking of him as a young man. He was already taller than Pomponi, and would soon be catching up with his father. Perhaps some of Publius's outgrown tunics could be made to last another season or two for Lucius, who was also growing up far too rapidly.

As if thoughts of them called them forth, the boys came racketing into her solar, shouting and playing at being invading Moors and Roman defenders. "I have you!" Publius shouted.

"Nay," cried Lucius, "You'll not take me alive! I am of solid Roman stock, and I'll stand fast to the end."

"So be it!" said Publius, drawing back a hand holding a stick from the wood supply as if to stab his brother.

But the hand is caught by a larger, stronger hand. "Hold, enough. Have a care with your younger brother, Publius. One day you may need him on a real battlefield. Wife, what is this unseemly racketing about? Where is that worthless Grammaticus? I paid good coin for him – 4,500 to be exact. If he does not prove worth his keep, I'll demote him to the field, so I will. A few days harvesting the grain will sharpen his attention."

"I am here, Master Publius, I am here!" A slender man with blond hair and blue eyes who resembled the statues one sometimes sees of winged Mercury hurried after the boys. "We were reviewing the late war in Hispania, and the reenactment grew a bit intense."

A tiny serving girl appeared at that moment. "Cook seths dat beckfust is weady," she lisped in her childish voice, "If it pwease you, sir and madam."

"Thank you, Blossom," Pomponi said. "We will be there directly." Then she addressed her husband and sons, "It will not go well this day if we keep Cook waiting. You know how temperamental he is. If we hope for an edible noonday meal, we had best attend his efforts."

"Of course," the elder Publius said. "Boys, go wash those grubby hands then join us hence at table. Grammaticus, see to it! These lads will be consuls one day; they need to learn manners as well as battle moves. M'lady wife?"

Publius offered his arm to his frail wife, who had never quite fully recovered from the difficult births of their two sons. She placed her hand upon his arm, and managed to rise gracefully from her seat at the loom, even though he could feel the strain in her as she rose. "With pleasure, m'lord husband."

They adjourned to the serving room, passing through the main room to get to it from Pomponi's solar. Breakfast was a rich barley porridge, laden with cream and honey. There was a fluffy mound of scrambled eggs, delicately spiced, a huge round of cheese, and a bowl of fresh figs. There was no meat with this meal; it was summer, and not yet the season of butchering. There was no practical reason to kill an animal for a simple family breakfast.

The boys came in from the courtyard, hands and faces conspicuously clean and the edges of their hair damp from their recent ablutions. They both looked a bit chastened, and approached the table with sober decorum, so it was relatively certain that the Grammaticus had given them both a good dressing down. Pomponi carefully did not notice the grass stains on Lucius's tunic or the mud on Publius's knees. Clearly, the morning lessons had been lively.

Little Blossom, the cook's baby daughter, waited upon the table with grave care – even though she could barely reach the tabletop. Publius deftly caught his cup, and did not chastise the little one for her efforts to wait table. Their household was a gracious one, rarely marred by internal strife. There was more than enough of war and conflict away from home.

The eggs were superb, and indeed would not have been edible had they delayed their meal. The cheese was new, and squeaked between their teeth as they ate it, but it was still good. The barley porridge was hot and deliciously sweet and rich. The boys dug into it with relish, while Publius savored the spicy eggs. Then he turned his attention to his wife, who was nibbling delicately at a fig.

"You are not eating much, my wife," he said gravely, "Are you unwell?"

"Just a touch of the old troubles," she said. They had both hoped for a large family, but her health had put an end to that dream. Still, he could not ask for a better helpmate, and although he could have put her aside for a more fertile woman, Publius valued her steady hand upon the estate during his inevitable absences.

"Try just a little of the egg, and a bit of the barley," he urged. "they are both quite good."

"Perhaps a bit of the barley porridge, but only a taste of the eggs. The spice upsets my stomach, you know."

Publius nodded. He did know, and had no desire to walk the halls that night with a woman groaning in pain. So, with his own hands, he dished a generous serving of the barley porridge and a small taste of the egg, and watched approvingly as she made the effort to eat. "The new cook is worth every penny we paid for him," he noted approvingly. "And it was worth the added cost to bring his family with him." Publius patted little Blossom on the head as she brought around a heaping tray of bread and butter. "Ah, that is very nice, little one," he approved. He then noticed that Lucius had one foot stuck out, just where it could trip the small girl. He fixed the boy with a glare, and Lucius looked properly ashamed and drew in his foot. Some masters would have encouraged such behavior and laughed uproariously at when the little one fell and even have punished her for clumsiness. Publius congratulated himself that he was not that sort of person. One never knows, he thought to himself, what fortunes might befall us tomorrow.

"He is, indeed," Pomponi replied, discovering that the porridge was just to her liking and beginning to eat it with some appetite.

She did not miss the little by-play between father and son. Publius Junior did not seem to notice it at all, but she was fairly certain that he did for he made sure to keep his own feet tucked in and gravely assisted their small waitress. Blossom was very much the household darling, and quite spoiled even with her new duties at table.

After breakfast, Publius decided that the Grammaticus deserved some time off after the lively morning study session, and took his two sons to the new fields at the edge of the estate. There, he put them to work at that perennial farmer's task of picking rocks and piling them at the edge of the field where they would be used to make walls. When the lads were well at work, he walked on over to one of the older fields to view the harvesting going on there. The slaves were hard at work under the supervision of Agrarius, a recently freed slave who continued to work on the estate for a small wage. In many ways, the man's lot was harder than it had been before, but he seemed to take pride in his condition as freedman and was a symbol of a possible future for all the slaves, if they worked hard and saved their earnings. Publius allowed each of them to keep a portion of any money earned by hiring out to the neighbors. These could be sturdy, loyal clients, as attached freedmen were called, in time.

Near the house, two clusters of workers were threshing the grain and separating the grain from the chaff. One group was flailing the ripe grain on the threshing floor, while another group was tossing the grain into the air and catching it is a basket. Just a little farther away, a small donkey was walking in an interminable circle while the clean kernels were poured onto the bowl of the stone grinder. There would be fresh bread and perhaps even sweet cakes. Publius savored the thought. In the far fields, he could see a man plowing, using an ard-type plow, drawn by one of his prize oxen. It was good to be home for a time – even if it turned out to be only a short while.

The work was going along well, and Publius picked a few ears of grain from the field to chew as he walked along to the sheep pasture. Here, the shepherd boy was tootling mournfully on a set of pipes while gazing off down the valley. He was mooning after one of the serving girls, but that was no excuse for not noticing the half-grown lambs that had just blundered into a thicket of briars. Publius cuffed the lad soundly, and then helped extract the foolish sheep.

By then, it was time for the midday meal. Publius walked back down the mountain, and shared a lunch of bread, cheese and cold spring water with his sons. One of the reasons he had chosen this land was for the cold water that bubbled up from a spring that ran the year around. It was one reason, he felt, that the workers and family who lived on the farm seemed to have better health than those who lived in the city.

When lunch was over, he showed his sons how to stack the stones, dry, into a wall and left them again to their task. His next stop was a lower field that was being plowed for a winter grain crop. He followed that up with checking on the new plantation of olive trees and grapes. He then returned to the boys, checked their work, praising them and correcting a couple of errors.

The three of them then returned to the house. Their evening meal was a frugal one by patrician standards. They had a freshly slain chicken, roasted and stuffed with savory grain. There were figs, of course, some new wine which was not bad, a crusty loaf of bread from the estate's bakery oven, along with more of the new cheese. There was a trifle made of almond paste, shaped into the form of a swan for dessert. This would have been Pomponi's contribution.

In addition to the sweet, Pomponi had a surprise for her menfolk. She had completed the tunics for Publius Senior and Junior, and had discovered that she even had a breadth left to make one tunic for Lucius. They declared the new garments very fine, and Publius said that when he took young Publius to visit the city, they would certainly wear them. He also made a mental note that he would take a full complement of the new guardsmen who were training; the city was a dangerous place, and the new garments would mark them out as being prosperous.

Rome in those days was a rabbit warren of alleyways, shops, and open air market places as well as the fine avenues with their rows of statues and elegant buildings. It would not do to relax his vigilance and lose his sons to some lowly footpad now that they were growing tall. Publius the elder smiled to himself. It would be a pleasure to take his two fine sons and show them off in the capital city, to watch their eyes grow round with wonder at all the sights and to share their excitement at the spectacles in the Forum.

Fictionalized? Absolutely, because we have almost no records at all of the Publius Cornelius household. Complete fiction? Not quite. We know that the records show a

Caesarian birth for son Publius, yet the family tree shows that both boys are sons of Pomponi. There are a number of possible answers for this: the records are simply exaggerated; there was a second wife, of whom there is no record; the boys might have been twins; or Lucius might have been the elder son. Since there is no recorded birthdate for either, Lucius might have been the younger son by minutes instead of years. We simply do not know the answers to these questions. Whatever records might have explained the mystery are long turned to dust.

What do we have left that show records of Roman life? We have inscriptions on tombstones and graphitti scratched on walls. We have mosaics showing scenes from domestic life. We have the hideous tragedy of Pompeii that left ready-made molds of volcanic ash for plaster casts of the people who died there, creating models that are so realistic we can see the agony etched on their faces. And we have the terrain, the foods that are still grown in the region and the knowledge that farming works pretty much the same way anywhere it is practiced. Oh, there are variations on themes – some areas are lucky enough not to have rocks to pick, but the Roman fields are not among them.

These things tell us of possible activities on a typical day in a patrician family setting. Some of the families became so obsessed with a display of status that they had a separate slave for every household function; but the Cornelii don't seem to be cut of that sort of cloth. They were military men, men who focused on duty to country and a degree of honor. I have chosen to think that Publius the father was capable of affection, that he cared for his estate, and that he acted as a father figure, not only to his two sons, but also the many people who lived and worked on his farm. Shall we say, feudalism at its finest rather than at its worst. History tends to bear this out, for subsequent events – which we will examine at greater length – indicate that Publius

Scipio, someday to become Africanus, had a deep and abiding affection for his father.

We also know that creating fabric was the primary preoccupation of women in Rome and in similar societies. This was a practical need, not some sort of vanity occupation. For example, in feudal England, each lordly household was obligated to provide two sets of clothing to each and every man and woman on the estate. Since spinning and weaving was all done by hand, the woman of the house and her ladies in waiting – often daughters of neighboring estates who were being fostered out – would spend many hours every day spinning and weaving. With the advent of weavers' guilds, this changed, and it became more of a display of a refined skill. But in the days of early Rome, the women's handiwork would still be needed.

Many of the serving people on an estate such as the one described here would have been slaves. Rome carried on a thriving slave trade. It was not limited to any one color or race, and its saving grace was that a slave could save up funds and buy his or her freedom. Theoretically, that is. Someone like the Grammaticus, whose purchase price was extremely high, might never manage his own purchase price.

Still, it was a busy, bustling world and flawed though it was, it laid the foundations for the formation of a democratic form of government. Publius had privilege, but he also had duties. He was obligated to be part of the governing body, and he was obligated to military service to his country. He would have been gravely concerned about the education of his sons, and he would have expected them to learn every aspect of life on the estate so that they could run it wisely when it became their turn to do so. And while he had the opportunity to do so, he would have wanted to look over his fields and farmlands, making sure that his people were all doing their jobs.

Rome was, at the time, a giant melting pot of cultures as her armies brought in new slaves, new prizes and new goods. It made no difference that the slaves were ripped from their homes, that the goods and gold had once belonged to someone else; this was the way that many nations operated at the time. It made Rome wealthy, bustling, and the Place to Be.

There were many other things going on in the world at the same time, but the Romans were oblivious to places and events that were beyond their very well-built roads and out of marching distance of their armies. Perhaps this is a good thing; who knows what might have happened if the Pax Romana had owned tanks and automatic weapons, airplanes and trains. Those things were left for a later war and a different conquering race.

As it was, they made their way as far southeast as Arabia and Northern Africa and as far northwest as the southern border of Scotland. For a culture that traveled on foot or horseback, that was an extensive amount of territory, essentially defining the area of the "known world." Spain, Gaul and Britain – that is, Wales and England, were gathered in, as were Syria and Israel. Carthage was one of the holdouts, and thereby will hang the rest of this tale because the military commander of Carthage and the military commander of Rome would make this conflict personal. Young Publius and young Hannibal would inherit their fathers' war, along with the charges from their fathers to each son to fight the other's culture for as long as they would live.

This enmity would drive Publius Cornelius Africanus's activities for most of the rest of his life, and would earn for him the last part of his name. But on this summer day, picking rocks or whatever other chores that a Roman place in the country required of a young patrician lad, he was a boy and would have been enjoying the activities of a lad of rank and privilege. He would be educated in the classical manner as well as in arms and armor, learning strategy, rhetoric and oration. Compared to hundreds of youngsters who lived in Rome itself and in the surrounding countryside, young Publius had it good.

With no birth control, babies proliferated. Unwanted infants were often exposed, frequently with a distinctive little necklace that would identify the child if he or she somehow managed to survive. In fact, it was a major theme of dramatic entertainment – the child that was exposed at birth, then turns up later just in time to inherit an estate or to save the family, identified by the baby necklace. Modern moms might wonder how any mother could possibly give up her baby, but the real truth is that women had no more rights than a prize mare. If the father did not approve the babe, out it went – usually before the mother was up and around and able to even arrange alternative custody for the infant. That has come up as a theme for legends as well – the Arthurian cycle, Moses, Osiris; that business of disposing of unwanted babies or hiding them has a lengthy history. New born humans are pretty short on self-defense.

But being exposed wasn't the only thing that could happen to infants in the days of the early Roman Empire. Sanitation was limited, even in the elegant homes of the rich. Fleas, lice, and vermin of all kinds abounded, as they do anywhere that large numbers of humans gather together, right along all the diseases that they spread. Those who could afford the trip would go to the country in the summer when disease was at its most rampant. But hundreds of migrants, slaves and other ordinary people would have to live through the Roman summer inside the city.

Other things could happen to children, as well. Rome might not have had automobiles, but it did have chariots, horses, ox carts, venders and sometimes panicked crowds. In the narrow, twisting streets of Rome a mob could and sometimes did lead to people being killed in the crush.

Children were expected to work and no allowance was made for their age or fragility. And some of those jobs would have had any modern Family Services department on the doorstep of the establishment with warrants and custody papers for the kids. Rome was exciting, but it wasn't safe.

It was a place where people could make futures or lose them, develop a wonderful life or wind up dead in an alley. It wasn't even all that safe for those who were in in the upper echelons. Power shifts, poisoning, assassination and more – Rome was a city of intrigue. Hollywood only publicized the most famous ones – as can be attested by the many gravestones with left-handed compliments to the deceased.

This was the city where Publius Cornelius planned to bring his oldest son for a visit. His father and grandfather had both been consuls there, and he had every expectation that he, himself, would one day hold office, and so would young Publius and perhaps Lucius also. It was the way it had been, and it was the way that it would always be. Publius Cornelius could envision no other possible course for his son and heir, or for his second son.

Chapter 2: Fireside Tales

Let us fast forward a few years. Publius and Lucius are both taller, their father has gone a bit gray and has picked up a few scars from battle. Their mother, although a little more fragile, still manages the estate. These days she is assisted by the Grammaticus who proved to be adept at record keeping and numbers – a skill he was teaching his young charges. Again, we are creating a fiction born of imagination, because there are no accounts of this time. However, story-telling has long been a favorite pastime of many cultures, and stories of famous ancestors always makes good telling. The setting here is fictional, but the story about the grandfather is drawn from history.

The family is gathered around the fireside. Little Blossom, now grown into a slender preteen, gracefully places apples on the hearth to bake, brings drinks and takes away the used cups and dishes.

"Tell us a story," Lucius begs his father.

"Yes, please tell us a story," Publius adds his voice to the plea.

"Well, I don't know," their father mused, "I hear that the Grammaticus had to wrest you from the dairy to attend your lessons this day."

Publius colored up like a girl. His father kept a straight face, and their mother bent her head over her sewing. Neither commented, but the father was sure that the mother was aware that the new dairy maid he had brought home as part of his spoils of war was a comely lass. "Please father," Publius's voice cracked and broke, and he cleared his throat and tried again. "Please, tell us a story. You are not home often now, and your stories are the best."

"Very well, that is a good point. What story would you like to hear?"

"Tell us about Grandfather Gnaeus and the first Roman navy," Lucius suggested.

"Ah, yes. Grandfather Gnaeus." Publius, the father, seemed to ponder for a moment. "Yes, I suppose that would be a good story." He settled himself back in his chair, and took up the pose that he always assumed before starting to tell a story.

This was the story that he told:

In your grandfather's time, you could stand on the shore near Reggio in the late evening, and if you looked across the waters, you could see the lights of Messina on the Island of Sicilia. Now, that would have been no great thing, but the other end of Sicilia stretched out toward Numidia. On that shore stands Carthage.

Now, the Carthaginians were great sailors in those days, and they had no trouble sailing over the waters to Sicilia, where they were rapidly claiming territory. Much alarmed, the citizens of Messina felt they had a choice of appealing to Syracuse or to Rome. Syracuse was already showing signs of waxing fat with power, so they called out to Rome as the lesser of two evils.

Rome hesitated. To come to Messina's aid, since she was not a Roman province, would constitute an act of war against Carthage. Carthage was not and is not a small power. Rome has fought its wars, but this one would not be on land – it would be on the sea. But after a time, Messina signed a treaty making it a Roman province. After that, there was no hesitation.

Appius Claudius, at the Ides of March at the beginning of his term of office (264 BC, for modern listeners to this tale) marched his men, double-time to the edge of the sea where allied ships were waiting. Before you could shout, "Cast off!" it seemed, they were across the strait and marching into Messina. Appius Claudius consolidated Messina's status as a province and his soldiers settled in to fortify the city and surrounding country side.

You may rest assured that Syracuse and Carthage certainly noticed this action. Although they had long been enemies, they at once made an alliance against Rome. Appius Claudius appealed to Hiero, the tyrant of Syracuse, to make a peace treaty. But Hiero would have none of it. Claudius was not one to sit about when there was an enemy to rout or work to be done, so he left a little housekeeping force in Messina and marched toward Syracuse. He made short work of them and then he tore into the Carthageans, routing their forces as well.

But then winter fell, and it was the season of Council. So nothing more was done at that time. In the spring, however, two consuls and their forces were dispatched – and Sicilia fell to the marching boots of Roman soldiers.

"But what about Grandfather?" Lucius piped up, his voice still a childish treble.

"I'm coming to that," Publius the father said. And the story went on.

Now, the combined forces of Manius Valerius and Octacilius Crassus marched across

Sicilia, having no trouble at all subduing the villages and settlements to the interior of that island. But the towns that lay on the seacoast were a different matter. No sooner did they think they had subdued one, but the Carthaginians supplied it from the sea, dashing in with their tall ships with five banks of oars, and leaving both supplies and men hauled from what seemed to be an endless supply from Carthage and Numidia.

Hiero of Syracuse, however, grew worried that while he was battling Rome, Carthage would nip in and steal victory from them both. So, like Messina, he decided that the Republic of Rome was a better choice as an ally than the Carthaginians, who were well known to be sharp traders and not above a little larceny on the side. So he sent a peace envoy to Valerius and Crassus, and they gladly drew up an agreement. Syracuse would have to pay an indemnity to Rome, but they would also have a staunch ally against Carthage.

Carthage did not like this alliance one little bit. They gathered mercenary forces and launched a vast navy and army which would land at Agrigento, an independent city-state that had been a protectorate of Carthage for some time. When 40,000 Carthaginian troops landed on Sicily, Rome – whose assembly had hoped their troubles were over – sat up and took notice.

"Was that when Grandfather ruled the navy?" Lucius asked. Publius, the son, covered his lower face with one hand, but gravely answered his brother, "Not quite yet. Stop interrupting or we'll never get there before bedtime."

Publius, the father, ignored this byplay, and went on with the story. By now, he had collected quite an audience, for this was a favorite tale and he was a good story teller.

The Roman armies descended upon Agrigento, but then things started to go wrong. Valerius and Crassus were not the best of generals, and they allowed the Carthageans to gather up all the food. Had not Hiero intervened, the Roman army would have starved to death before the city they were besieging gave up for lack of food. But Hiero was an honest tyrant; once he made a bargain, he kept it.

"Is that when…" Lucius started, but his brother put one hand on his arm, and he subsided.

Now, it just so happened – as I think I mentioned before – that many of the Carthaginian forces were mercenaries. When the provisions grew too thin, one night they all sneaked out to the ships and sailed away, leaving Agrigento undefended. With no army left, Agrigento surrendered. The Romans enslaved and sold most of the population – but they were purchased by the people of Syracuse with the understanding that the money would be paid back later. But that action did not make the other small cities love Rome. It was a bad decision on the part of Valerius and Crassus.

For the next few years, Sicily became the chew-bone in a tug-of-war between Rome and Carthage. Rome was superb on land, but Carthage had a masterful command of the sea. A Carthaginian saying was that Rome could not wash its hands in the Mediterranean without Carthage's permission. But that was about to change.

In all of these battles, a Roman force managed to capture a quinquereme – one of the tall ships used by the Carthaginians and the Phoenicians – that being the name for the people of the greater area around Carthage.

Carthage had 120 quinqueremes. With them, they ruled the seas. Rome had never made ships before, but they had captured a quinquereme in Messina. They carefully took it apart, piece by piece, copied the parts and made ships. They built a model on land, and hired instructors from neighboring lands to teach their land bound people how to row. By spring, Rome had a navy of 100 quinqueremes and two hundred triremes.

"Now it is time for Grandfather!" Lucius burst out, unable to contain himself.

Publius, the father, hid a smile. "Yes, my son. Now it is time for Grandfather."

Gnaeus Cornelius Scipio had a solid reputation as a general on land, but he had never commanded a force at sea. He took his army overland to Reggio, and crossed safely into Messina. However, the navy had to travel by sea, and with such a rabble of inexperienced sailors mixed with a few experienced hands, some of the ships made better time than others. Grandfather Gnaeus didn't want to sit around and do nothing while he waited for the rest of the fleet to catch up.

So he took the seventeen ships that he had, and headed out to Lipari, thinking that if he captured that island he would secure a shipping lane for Rome. He didn't have a bit of trouble taking Lipari, which is a tiny island after all, but he forgot one small detail.

Publius, the father, paused dramatically for his audience to fully appreciate the moment.

With only twenty warships, the Carthaginian navy swooped down in the night and blocked the entrance to the harbor. When morning came, there was nothing to do but surrender the ships. The crews fled into the hills, but Gnaeus Cornelius Scipio and most of his army were captured.

"Oh, poor Grandfather!" Lucius breathed.

"Not one of his finer moments, for sure," Publius the father smiled. "But all was not lost, and a lesson learned. Carthage was so intent on capturing your grandfather and his seventeen ships that while they were distracted the other 283 ships with their cargo of sailors and soldiers sailed into Messina without losing a single one. As for your grandfather, he was traded to Rome in a prisoner exchange, and six years later was elected consul again."

The audience clapped in enthusiastic approval.

"But what happened, then, Father?" young Publius asked. "Surely those ships and men did not just sit there in dock."

"You are quite right, young Publius," his father replied. "They certainly did not. With your grandfather captured, Gaius Duilius was left not only in charge of the army, but of the navy also. He reasoned that since the Carthaginians were so agile at sea, that it was best to slow them down a bit. So he invented a thing called "the raven.""

Now the Raven was an interesting contraption. It fastened onto the mast of the ship, near the prow of the boat. The ship could then be aimed at another ship, head on, and when it got close enough for ramming the Raven would drop its beak onto the other ship. This would hold it fast so that it could not get away allowing the army to get on board and take over the ship. As you all well know, the Roman army is very good in close quarter combat; this would give the Romans an advantage over the troops from Carthage who might be good at sailing, but were out of practice in real battle.

Gaius Duilius equipped all of his ships with a raven. He sailed out of Messina, looking for trouble – hopefully in the form of the Navy from Carthage. His hopes were answered, for he soon met a wide line of 100 quinqueremes. The Carthaginian troops shouted with derision as they saw the awkward line of Roman ships advancing toward them. But soon their shouts turned to dismay, for the Roman ships came faster and faster, not caring if they broke their prows by ramming into the ships from Carthage. Worse yet for the Carthaginians, when a Roman ship came within ramming distance, it dropped a raven on the opposing ships deck. As soon as the raven held the ship secure, battle hardened fighters boiled over the railings onto the deck, dealing death and mayhem to those aboard. Three thousand Carthaginians died and seven thousand were taken prisoner. Better yet, thirty of the Carthagean ships were captured, including the flagship, and fifteen of them were sunk.

Now, the applause burst out full of enthusiasm, for none of this household – save the new milkmaid – had come from regions that supported the Phoenicians or their primary city, Carthage.

When the applause had died down, young Publius, eyes shining with patriotic fervor said, "But that wasn't the end of it, was it father."

"No," his father said, "There is still plenty of opportunity for brave deeds and marvels of generalship. Rome immediately set about making more ships, for if there is one thing we do well it is making things. When Carthage heard of this, they swore that no Roman soldier would set foot on African soil.

The next spring, Rome set out with 230 galleys; Carthage met them, already in battle formation, with 250 ships. The superior force bore down on the Roman ships in an arc-shaped line divided into thirds. The center would take out the main force of the ships, and the sides would then wrap around the flanks and surround the opposing ships.

But, oh, did they ever get a surprise! The Romans met them with a wedge formation, the supply ships and the slower moving vessels at the rear, positioned in the wide part of the V shape. But also back there was a third of the military vessels to protect the transport craft. The Carthageans expected to quickly subdue the inexperienced sailors, but they were met with such ferocity that the center of their line could not hold and began to retreat. But instead of chasing them, the two forward lines of the V wrapped back around, and attacked the flanking ships that were launching an offensive against the transport ships!

The ships from Carthage that were nearest the open sea were able to get away, but the ones that were nearest the Sicilian shore were cut off.

The Romans lost twenty-four ships that day, but the thirty of the Carthagean ships were sunk and sixty-three of them captured.

Again there was applause. Even their mother, who was often quiet at such times clapped her hands together in praise of the event and of the story-teller, upon whom she looked with quiet pride.

Then she said, "It is time for me to retire. Do not stay up too late, my sons. Tomorrow is another day, with many things to do." She did not say it, but it hung there in the air: the knowledge that one day, before too long, these two sons would follow their father into battle for the honor of Rome.

Thus, we spin another fictionalized tale of an event that could have happened in the household of Publius Cornelius Scipio. The story of the naval battles are a matter of history – it seems that keeping record of such things was more important than records of fashion of the day, or the scandals that might have surrounded the rich and famous. Did such an evening occur? We will never know. But it might have. Publius, the father, was trained in oration as were all patricians of the day. Story-telling is an art found in many cultures, and a way of instructing the young. With no television, winter evenings could become long – story telling was a favorite event in many cultures until the boxed vacuum tube brought a different kind of story telling into our living rooms.

But now you, as well as the boys and servants of that long ago household (even if we see it in our imagination) know of the events that began the Punic Wars and that would become a driving force in two military households.

Indeed, all households of Rome with men between the ages of 18 and 46 could be said to be military households. Military service was expected of all able-bodies men, and there could be no social or political advancement without it.

If a young man entered as a cavalryman, he could expect his service to be only two years long. The reason for this was because of the financial cost. A cavalryman would be expected to provide his own horse, and to bring a slave or servant to help care for the horse. This expense also effectively kept those of lower ranks from entering the cavalry.

An infantryman, on the other hand, would be expected to serve for 20 years. They would be organized into legions. Each legion would be composed of 4,000 infantry – except in times of war when they would number 5,000. Each legion was divided into 10 cohorts, numbered according to their length of service. The commander in charge of the highest numbered cohort would be in charge of the legion. The troops were of mixed ages; an arrangement designed to allow the older, more experienced soldiers to assist the newer ones and keep up their moral. They were also there to step into gaps in the ranks should a soldier fall. Keeping the phalanx even and moving was an important part of infantry combat.

Weapons included short swords, and a pair of javelins. By way of defense, they had body armor and shields. When compared to the foot soldiers, the cavalry were lightly armed and armored. Their best defense was speed.

The Roman army was motivated by civic duty and patriotism. They knew that great or small, they would be honored for their service when they returned home. The sons of first families knew that they would be expected to serve Rome in the Senate and possibly in some civil duty between their bouts of service in the army itself.

Chapter 3: The Young Soldier

Indeed, it would not be long before young Publius would be setting out on his own military ventures. But before we take a good look at his adventures, we need to visit Carthage for a short while.

The Barca family was the Carthaginian counterpart to the Cornelius family. Hamilcar Barca took command of the military forces of Carthage in Sicily at around age 30, in the year 247 BC – nearly 17 years after Grandfather Gnaeus' ignominious defeat. Hamilcar also fathered a son that year, and named him Hannibal.

Hamilcar was an able general, and had he been provided the support he deserved, that might well have ended this tale before it began. But like many other nations before that time and since, Carthage was divided politically. On the one hand, Phoenician ships traded all across the known world. They ventured as far north as Denmark, and far down the western coast of Africa. But on the other hand, they were able farmers and had learned the best ways to take advantage of their local environment. The two factions were – as one might readily suppose – in opposition. The farmers preferred to keep the armies at home, isolating the country. The traders wanted expansion. After all, the farther the reach of Carthaginian borders, the greater their trading area. The Hanno clan was isolationist being composed primarily of those with agrarian interests, and the Barca clan expansionist and interested in trading. With all of the opposition at home, Hamilcar Barca was given only two legions with which to manage Sicily.

With such a small force, Hamilcar elected to establish his military base atop Monte Pellegrino, where he could see all of Palermo. From this vantage point, he could view Roman maneuvers, including any approaching ships from the sea. The location gave the defenders the advantage, and from time to time Hamilcar's forces would sally forth to conduct guerilla raids on the rearguard of the Roman army as they lay siege to Marsala. When the Romans attacked his position on Monte Pellegrino, he handily defeated them.

For four years, this stalemate continued. Hamilcar expected the Romans to sue for peace. But they used a different strategy. Having observed that Hamilcar's position was unassailable by force, they decided to cut his supply lines. However, this involved preventing ships from sailing in with supplies, and that meant that Rome would have to reconstitute its navy. By now, their current ships were in bad shape and that meant that they would need to build at least 200 new quinqueremes. The Roman treasury was all but empty, and they did not want to levy a new general tax or ask their allies to help defray the cost. Instead, they issued war bonds and required land owners, members of the Senate and public officials to purchase them. After the conflict was ended (hopefully with lots of booty) those who had purchased bonds would be able to redeem them.

In the spring, Carthaginian ships sailed toward Sicily. But this was not a fighting force – they had grown contemptuous of Roman seamanship. It was essentially a supply convoy, intended to bring troops and supplies to Hamilcar.

The wind had favored the Carthaginian ships. As the Romans sailed out from some small islands, the wind drove the ships from Carthage straight into the Roman fleet. The fighting was fierce, but as had happened before, once the situation moved from being maneuvers at sea into hand-to-hand combat, the Romans excelled. The ships from Carthage were saved by a shift in the wind that enabled flight back to Carthage. Once there, the commander in charge of the ships was crucified for his defeat.   At this point, Carthage ordered Hamilcar to petition Rome for peace. The terms of the treaty called for complete withdrawal of all Carthaginian forces from Sicily, and for Carthage to pay 2,200 talents to Rome in installments over ten years. In return, Rome would allow Carthage to remain independent. However, the Roman Senate was not pleased with this battlefield decision. They dispatched a committee of ten to further assess the situation. However, upon arrival, the committee concurred that Catulus, the Roman general who had drafted the treaty, was correct in his assessment of the situation. The only change they made was to raise the yearly payment to 3,200 talents, with the added 10,000 talents to be paid in a lump sum as soon as the treaty took effect. In addition, the small islands around Sicily would also come under Roman control.

Thus ended the First Punic War, in 241 BC, a conflict that had lasted for twenty-three years – time enough for a lad to grow into a man. One might have expected some years of peace to follow. Such was not the case.

Carthage refused to pay the mercenaries that had made up a great part of its army. Instead, its officials argued that they had fought only half a year, and would therefore be paid only half that sum. To make a fairly long story short, Hamilcar was given the task of defeating the rebellious mercenaries. At first he was lenient with them; but when they cut the hands, feet, ears and nose off an emissary and buried him alive, Hamilcar proved his efficiency as a military commander. He drove them up onto a little hill, fenced them in and held them there until they resorted to cannibalism, eating their prisoners and slaves. They sent out a party to request peace, but Hamilcar killed them.

The besieged rebels took this to mean that the diplomatic party had defected, and they attacked. That was all that Hamilcar needed. He sent in the elephants, drove the rebel army into a little depression, and they were trampled to death. That went a long way to restoring order at home for Carthage.

With Sicily and its surrounding islands in Roman hands, the expansionist Barcas turned their eyes toward Spain. Spain was a rich prize, with natural resources, gold mines and more. Legend has it, that as Hamilcar was preparing for departure, Hannibal – who would have been around nine years old at the time – begged to go with his father, brothers, brother-in-law, and uncles. Hamilcar, apparently spotting an opportunity, is said to have placed his son's hand upon the animal being sacrificed to Baal in preparation for the trip, and said to him: "Swear, my son, that you will never be amicus to Rome." Now some translations say that this meant that he swore his son to eternal enmity toward Rome, while Livy wrote that Hannibal was never to be a friend to Rome. But "amicus" also meant ally or subject of Rome. Since Rome's habits of acquisition were well known around the Mediterranean, it is entirely possible that Hamilcar's primary purpose would have been to keep Carthage out of the hands of the ever-spreading Roman empire. How did Polybius and

Livy learn of this? Well, it seems that many years later, Hannibal was in exile at the court of Antiochus III. He was age 54, and needed some sort of proof that he was a reliable ally against Rome, and told the story of his oath at that time.

In the year 229, Hamilcar died in battle, and Hasdrubal took over the invasion of the Iberian (Spanish) peninsula. Hannibal, who was by now a young man aged somewhere between 18 and 25 years, ably aided his brother-in-law, Hasdrubal, in the conquest. Hannibal's brothers, Hasdrubal and Mago also were in command of portions of the Carthaginian forces in Spain. They establish a strong presence in Spain.

Meanwhile, Rome was not idle. It annexed Sardinia and Corsica, further consolidating its own presence in the Iberian Peninsula. In 226, the Ebo or Ibrus river was established as a boundary between the territory gained by these two warring superpowers. In 221, Hasdrubal fell in battle, and command of the Carthaginian forces was taken up by Hannibal.

In 220, the people of Spain appealed to Rome for assistance against this brash young general. According to treaty, the river Ebo divided Spain into Carthaginian territory and Roman territory. But the city Seguntum, located on the Ebo, was essentially a Roman city.

In spring 219, Hannibal attacked Seguntum, and laid siege to it for eight months. In November, it fell to the armies from Carthage. This had Rome's attention. The conflict broke the treaty made at the end of the First Punic War, and also violated the agreement that the Ebo would be the boundary. Rome declared war.

Unfortunately, the lack of help from Rome and the punitive sacking by the Carthage armies had the Iberian people's attention also. Raw and angry, they whipsawed back and forth between supporting one side or the other. Meanwhile, other subjugated states noticed how little and how late the support from Rome, and added their own restiveness to the situation. In fact, when asked to support Rome by resisting Hannibal's armies, the Gauls laughed so uproariously, wrote Livy, that the elders and the marshals had a hard time quieting them.

When lots were drawn for the various areas needing Roman legions sent out with consuls, Publius Scipio Cornelius and his brother Gnaeus drew Spain. Publius was diverted to Northern Italy where the Gauls were staging an uprising, and Gnaeus went on to Spain. This was in 218, after the fall of Seguntum. It was also in 218 that Hannibal would take his elephants, which had proven to be a supreme tactical asset, over the Alps, thus allowing him to attack the Romans on Italian soil, in an area where they had always thought that the geography would protect them.

No one is quite sure exactly where he crossed the Alps. It is known that on the way up, the mountain dwellers rolled rocks down on his army, and generally harassed them. But once they entered the pass, and started down the other side, they were left alone. On the Italian side, their greatest challenges were the weather and rockslides. Two major avalanches had blocked the way, and it took several days to build a space wide enough for horses and elephants to traverse. By the time Hannibal's army reached the more hospitable plain, his elephants were in sad shape.

In 218 BC, Publius Scipio Cornelius, the father of Publius Scipio Africanis the Elder, and his brother Gnaeus were sent to Spain with the Roman armies to put a stop to the advance of Hasdrubal and Mago, Hannibal's brothers. However, there was a Gallic uprising in northern Italy, and Publius delayed to help put it down while Gnaeus went on to Spain.

The Battle of Ticinus

Seventeen-year-old Publius Scipio (someday to be Africanis) was with his father's army. Publius Scipio Cornelius left his son in the company of a seasoned cavalry unit – possibly for the lad's safety. But seeing his father and uncle about to be killed, young Scipio rallied his cavalry unit and led a charge to rescue them both. This story was told to Polybius by Laelius. Laelius was said to be a close friend and comrade to Publius Scipio, as well as his able lieutenant.

As we have in earlier chapters, let us imagine what it might have been like at that battle.

In the early dawn hours, near the banks of the Ticinus, Publius Scipio watched his father and uncle organize the troops, giving them instruction. All about him, men were gearing up – as were he and his friend, Laelius. First they donned their regular tunics. Then, they added a wool tunic – in Publius Scipio's case, woven by his mother's handmaiden, little Blossom who had grown up to be a lovely woman. His mother had in recent years become too frail to manage the big loom, and confined her work to fine linens woven on a much smaller loom. The wool tunic would absorb perspiration and cushion their bodies from chafing. They draped a scarf around their necks – again to protect their skin from the metal cuirass. Publius and Laelius helped each other into their cuirasses, checking to make sure that the lacings and buckles were secure. About their waists they fastened the baltea, a leather belt which would hold up the balteus – a weighted leather apron intended to protect the groin – as well as the sheath for their short swords. Their sandals had nails embedded in the outer sole, intended to dig into the earth for better traction. Shin guards helped to protect their legs. They checked the inner sole of each shoe carefully to see if an added layer of leather was needed. Those nails hurt if they wore through, even if it was the flat blunt end of them.

Because they would be on horseback, Publius and Laelius carried small, round shields and short spears.

As dawn broke, and after a bit of shouting, the armies clashed. As the day wore on, the lads could see from their vantage point in the rear guard that fewer and fewer men were standing on either side. Although the Cornelii brothers had started out in two separate units, as the fighting wore on, they drew closer and closer until their units were side by side, and then back to back. Suddenly, their standard bearer went down, and the fighting grew intense. Publius Scipio saw his father fall, and he could bear it no longer!

With a shout, he alerted his unit and they plunged boldly into the fray, jabbing with their wicked little spears and blocking blows with their small, round shields. Publius and Laelius rode to the center of the knot of fighting men and took up the older Publius and Gnaeus on their horses. The men were sorely wounded and bleeding, as were many of the soldiers with them. The fighters, both foot soldiers and cavalry, formed up around the leaders. Step by step they worked their way out of the center of the fighting.

And now, a return to recorded history.

With their leaders severely wounded, the Roman army began a strategic retreat back across the Po river to Placentia. Hannibal taunted them, inviting further combat, but the senior Publius refused to engage. The Gallic unrest was too great. Nearly 2,000 Gallic and Celtic conscripts deserted and joined the Carthaginians.

Perhaps it was at this point that, wounded, weary and disheartened, the older Publius begged an oath from the younger one, an oath that said he would always fight against Carthage, even unto death, and that he would forever defend Rome. Or perhaps that is the story the son told later, to explain his enmity toward the Barcas. It is said that, years later, when Publius Scipio heard that his father and uncle had, fallen in battle that he wept, screamed at the gods, and swore vengeance.

Legend is somewhat unclear on this point, but it is fairly certain that the encounter at Ticinus was Publius Scipio's, someday to become

Africanis, first encounter with Hannibal. It would certainly not be his last.

Over the next four or five years, it is certain that he, his father and his uncle were deeply involved in the Roman endeavors to hold back this aggressive young military genius. At the time of the **Battle of Trebia,** since Scipio Cornelius had been wounded in the battle at Ticinus, Sempronius had been sent to take his place and was the general in charge. This was music to Hannibal's ears because he felt more confident of his ability to trick Sempronius.

Hannibal had his younger brother Mago hide his troops in the thick brush along the Trebia River. There was a clear plain behind the brush, which at first glance would appear to be empty. At dawn, the Hannibal's Numidian cavalry attacked the Roman encampment. The Romans, roused from sleep, hastily formed up and turned the defense into an offense. The Numidians rode across the Trebia, and the Romans followed in hot pursuit. Sempronius ordered the men to wade river to pursue the fleeing cavalry.

Wet, cold, and hungry, the Roman soldiers were also engaged in an uphill battle, coming up from the river as they were. Now, Hannibal brought up the rest of his troops, with his elephants positioned in front of his cavalry where they could do the most good. This was one of the Roman's first encounters with Hannibal's elephants. The elephants rendered the unaccustomed horses in the Roman cavalry useless. The terrified animals broke from the control of their riders, dashing about and creating almost as much carnage as the elephants themselves. The Romans were at a supreme disadvantage. They would either have to retreat into the freezing cold waters of the Trebia or they would have to meet Hannibal's warm, dry and well-fed troops head on. Sempronius urged his troops forward, pushing at the center of Hannibal's line as was the custom of Roman troops of the day – a tactic Hannibal would use against them over and over.

As soon as they were well engaged, Mago's troops rose up from the bushes where they had been concealed, trapping the unfortunate men between two battle ready forces. Sempronius had taken nearly 40,000 men into the fray, but only about 10,000 survived to return to their camp at Placentia.

This debacle caused the Romans to have to raise a new level of 30,000 men to replace those lost to Hannibal's trickery. It almost seemed as if he had an endless supply of men, even though he was actually out of touch with Carthage. The reality was that Hannibal had lost scarcely any men at Trebia, although he had lost most of his elephants.

Tricking the Roman army seemed so easy to him. Soon, he discovered another place where he could set up an ambush.

The battle of Lake Trasimene

This one he set up based on what he knew about the opposing Roman general, Flaminius. Flaminius was known to be impulsive and to plunge in without thinking – particularly if he was angry. Hannibal knew just the way to do it. He also hoped to show the natives that Rome could not protect its allies. To do this, he rampaged around the countryside burning buildings and killing the livestock. He did not succeed in winning the people to his side, but he certainly enraged Flaminius.

On a misty May morning, Hannibal lured Flaminius into pursuing his army down a narrow path that lead onto a small plain beside the lake. Previously, Hannibal had stationed more troops in the corners of the plain, where they could not be readily seen. Once Flaminius forces were committed, Hannibal made short work of them, slaying nearly 15,000 of them – including the commander, Flaminius. Only 6000 Romans escaped.

Emboldened by his successes, Hannibal set up for what would be his greatest triumph on Roman soil: **The Battle of Cannae.**

The Roman troops at Cannae had been under the generalship of Lucius Amelius Paulus and Caius Terentius Varro. General Paulus fell in battle and it was under Varro that the armies made their retreat.

There are many accounts of the Battle of Cannae – with conflicting tales, and varied numbers. But on some things those accounts do agree. Hannibal had swelled the numbers of his troops by recruiting Spaniards, Gauls and Celts who had reason to detest the invading Romans. He was not relying on mercenary troops who would desert if they were not paid, or if the profits were exceeded by losses. But there were two things working against him. First, he had taken considerable losses in his journey over the Alps – his surviving elephants were sick and weak. Then he had lost more elephants at Trebia. Men and horses had also fallen on that journey, and at each battle – although his losses were small compared to those of Rome – he did lose men at each battle. Second, when he sent to Carthage for reinforcements and supplies, his request was refused. He was, therefore, unable to muster the men or supplies to lay siege to large cities. Instead, he had to rely on harrying tactics to wear down the Roman forces.

At Cannae, he filled the center ranks with Gauls – whom he fully expected to give way when confronted with the well-trained Roman legions. When they did, Hannibal's seasoned troops emerged from the bushes on both sides of the committed force. Perhaps if Paulus had been a more astute general or if the Roman army had not been riddled by desertions, the outcome might have been different. But as it was, the forces commanded by Paulus and Varro were caught between the jaws of the Carthaginian army, and only a few were fortunate enough to survive.

Who knows how history might have changed had Hannibal been adequately supplied and supported. In spite of his requests, Carthage sent only small amounts of supplies and few reinforcements. In spite of the victory at Cannae, Hannibal continued to make small sorties, keeping the Roman consuls busy putting out small brush fires, as it were.

At the Battle of Cannae – a dreadful loss for the Romans and a triumph for Hannibal – in 216, young Scipio served as a military tribune. At the end of the disaster, he escaped to Canusium with 4,000 other survivors. Legend has it – as told by Laelius to Polybius – that after the battle he came upon a group of young noblemen who were planning to defect.

Now, it had come to be said that young Publius Scipio was an orator of some extreme talent, as well as being well trained in the martial arts. He first held this group of would-be deserters at sword point. One does wonder how he was able to do that since the sword is hardly a distance weapon and can only target one man at a time. Perhaps he collared the leader of the group, and in that manner held sway. Or perhaps he cornered them in a room, and held the doorway against their leaving.

But however he did that, he managed to gain the group's attention, and then he began to orate. He threatened, he cajoled, he appealed to their pride. By the end of his speech, he not only made them all swear never to desert Rome, but to slay any man they might find who was similarly inclined. It should be noted that this was standard policy for Roman troops, but in the desperate moments at the end of the Battle of Cannae, it might have been understandable that some would turn faint of heart. It is said that the Romans lost some 44,000 troops in that battle, downed by the military prowess of Hannibal.

The real significance of Cannae was the lesson that Scipio learned from post-battle examination of Hannibal's tactics. Rome had entered the field of battle at Cannae with the superior force – 50,000 men to Hannibal's 40,000. Hannibal had become quite a thorn in Rome's side, and Rome was responding in its usual way – by sending in an overwhelming number of troops.

Hannibal had combined force with sweet-talk and promises, and had taken over a large portion of northern Italy following his daring foray over the Alps. By the time of the battle of Cannae, the Romans were truly worried that the daring young general would march on Rome itself. They did not know that he was limiting himself to wearing them down because he was receiving very little support from home. Hannibal knew very well that he did not have the forces needed to either take the city or hold onto it afterward should he have succeeded. But that didn't keep him from entertaining the Roman's attention with his antics.

His battle plan at Cannae took full advantage of Roman hubris and the general's need for a big win. By positioning his weakest troops in the middle, Hannibal drew in the Roman troops which were arranged in traditional fashion which was to place the light infantry in front, then to follow it up with the heavier infantry, with the cavalry on the flanks where they were more maneuverable.

By placing his weakest troops in the center of his forward line, Hannibal cozened the Roman commanders into thinking that they were winning, and they pressed forward. By the time they realized that it was a trap, their men were already deeply committed, and because of the traditional arrangement, they were unable to pull back. Thus, they were trapped by the pincers of the reserves that Hannibal had positioned on both sides of the field.

Scipio learned his lesson from this knavish tactic. Hannibal's combined approach of espionage and trickery were serving him very well, despite having to swell the ranks of his army by converting the Gauls. These were maneuvers that Scipio would use in Spain and then take with him to Africa, where he would turn the tables on the Carthaginians.

In many ways, Hannibal, ten years Scipio's senior, was very much his instructor in tactics. Scipio talked with soldiers, read reports and in all ways studied the methods that Hannibal was using to wear down the Romans.

However, not all the Romans were as easy to take in as Sempronius, Flaminius and Aemilius. Fabius, who had been observing Hannibal's tactics now began what might best be described as a war of attrition. He harried Hannibal with small battles, cut off his supplies, and refused to give him rest. Following the Battle of
Cannae and well into the latter years that Hannibal was in Italy, Fabius kept up these tactics, earning him the title of Cunctator or Delayer. Fabius kept up these tactics for twelve years. It was only toward the end that he became impatient, and that proved to be his undoing. But more of that later.

A small side note, which has little to do with the main theme concerns a siege of a major city in Sicily. Hiero, the ruler of Syracuse, had long been an ally of Rome. But upon his death, he was succeed by his grandson, Hieronymus. Hieronymus allied himself with Carthage. Marcellus, the governor of Sicily became alarmed by the pro-Carthaginian faction. When Hieronymus tried to rouse the neighboring city of Leontini, Marcellus immediately took notice. Syracuse closed its doors to him, and he laid siege there.

Now, here is the truly interesting bit. Many of the siege engines invented in Syracuse during 214-212 were designed by Archimedes, the mathematician who said, "Give me a fulcrum, a lever and a place to stand and I will move the world." When the siege ended, Archimedes was killed because he was too busy with a mathematical problem to follow the directions given to him for surrender.

Whether that was truly why he did not give himself up or whether there was some other reason, it still makes an interesting story.

Chapter 4: The Quaestorship

Publius Scipio returned to Rome after Cannae. Somehow, in spite of the dreadful defeat, Scipio was now considered a hero. The records are sparse for his civilian life, and like much of our quest into his history, must rely on small clues and general knowledge about the times. It is known that he was wed to Aemilia, daughter of Aemilius Paulus, the consul who fell at Cannae. Precisely when they were wed is not known, although it is a matter of record that they had two sons and two daughters.

Scipio organized games in honor of his father and uncle, and threw himself into them with gusto. Perhaps he met Aemilia there, and the two were drawn together in their mutual grief; or, perhaps they had been betrothed by their fathers before the battle. In any event, they were wed, and for a year or two Scipio led a civilian life.

When he was only twenty-four, he was elected curule aedile. There were two curule aedile in Rome. They oversaw other officials, such as the ones in charge of weights and measures. The lesser aediles kept order in the streets, looked after the market and in general functioned much like the police of today. The two curule aediles functioned somewhat like chiefs of police. The senate was not particularly happy about his election. They pointed out his youth, saying he was too young for the position. To this he pertly replied, "If all of Rome has voted for me, then I am old enough."

It is likely that it was during these years that he began his family. Apparently, he did quite well for himself in those days, and during the years when he returned to military life. Certain accounts say that when the lady Ameilia Tertia (she was the third child of Amelius) went to the temple to make sacrifices that she carried fine vessels for the sacrifice, such as gold rimmed crystal goblets. She would bear four children to Scipio – two sons and two daughters.

Let us again turn in imagination to what it must have been like for her, this Amelia Tertia. Women in Rome were so little valued that they were given a family name and a number. Ameilia was the third daughter of the Amelius who fell at Cannae – Tertia means three. Marriage to Publius Scipio, who was quite the rising young star in Rome at that time, would have meant both status and security.

As a military daughter, having recently lost both father and the man who would have been her father-in-law, she certainly would have been aware of the fragility of human life. At the same time, as a young woman with little family support, she would have been aware of the need to support her husband's position in the city. By dressing in her very best, and having a fine retinue of servants carrying fine vessels to the temple not only indicated her supplication of the gods, it helped show that her husband was generous to her and showed her support of him.

Let us further suppose, that a certain young woman named Blossom had been given to young Publius Scipio's household as a wedding gift, and that she was part of that fine procession. Keep in mind that Blossom is primarily a figment of this writer's imagination, but there is a reason for including her here – of that we will say more later.

Amelia's visits to the temples would have been an important part of her daily life. Not only did the size and quality of her retinue proclaim her place in Roman society, she might very well have believed that performing the rituals and sacrifices would help keep Publius safe when he was away with the military, or even when he was patrolling the streets of Rome. As previously mentioned, Rome was exciting, but it wasn't safe.

Amelia might have visited one of several temples to show her devotion and to perform rituals for the safety of her husband. For example, she might have visited Janus, the two-faced god who faced both the past and the future. Janus governed all change, and opened doors to all possibility. While Rome was at war, the door to Jupiter's temple would be open. She might have made offerings in memory of her father, and again for the safety of her husband. She might have visited Hera's temple – particularly if she desired a child. Certainly, she would have wanted one since a husband could divorce a wife who either bore no children or did not give birth to a son. Such devotion would have been expected of her. Wearing fine robes, having beautiful vessels for he sacrifices – these would all have been showing respect. She knew the risks that her husband faced.

For just a moment, let us imagine her robed in her finest clothing. The clothing for Roman women was strictly regulated until 195 BC, so her choices would have been limited. First, she would have had on a peplos or a chiton. These were garments made from two squares of cloth that were sewn up the sides, almost to the top. They were then – in the case of the peplos – fastened with pins to form short sleeves, or in the case of the chiton, long sleeves. Married women were entitled to wear the stola, although it was not required. Finally, there was the palla, a long cloak that respectable women wore when they went outside.

Since Aemilia was clearly a respectable young married woman, she would have been likely to wear her stola and palla over her peplos. Each of these garments would have been of fine cloth since her husband was well off financially. Perhaps her peplos would be linen or silk; her stola would be made from virgin wool as tradition demanded. The Palla might have been made of silk or wool, depending upon the season, and might have been decorated with a fringe or with fine trim along the edges.

The women and men servants in her retinue would also have been well dressed, although perhaps not in such finery as she herself wore. Accounts describing her procession include mention of fine crystal and gold trim on the sacrificial vessels. But for all her finery, one has to wonder what might have been her frame of mind. Having lost her father to the war, what were her feelings about sending her husband into that fray. Would her attitude be "with your shield or on it" or would she have been more deeply worried about his safety? Either way, it didn't really matter. When the time came he would have to go.

In 211, Scipio's Uncle Gnaeus and his father were slain in the battle at Ilourgeia, according to some accounts. It is probable that the front in Hispania had been starved of materials and manpower in favor of dealing with the Sicilian front throughout 213 and 212. But the Carthaginian forces had been steadily strengthened, and now included three able generals: Mago and Hasdrubal Barca, Hannibal's brothers, as well as Hasdrubal Gisco. Publius and Gnaeus decided to split their forces. Publius would take two thirds of their force against Mago and Hasdrubal Barca, while Gnaeus would take the remaining third and the Celtiberian allies against Hasdrubal Gisco. Perhaps they under estimated the might of the various generals, or perhaps they were just that desperate. Any modern participant of strategy or role playing games could have instructed them about the dangers of splitting your forces, and thus dividing your strength – but such commenters would have the advantage of historical perspective supplied by generations of critics.

The difficulties began almost immediately. Publius and his troops were constantly beset by Numidian cavalry under the direction of Masinissa, a Numidian prince who had been driven out of his homeland by his brother prince, Syphax. Publius had advanced as far as Urso, when he heard that the Spanish chieftain Andobales or Indibilis as he is sometimes called, was approaching with a force of 7500. Publius took a group of men on a forced night march to try to head off the added group before they could join the Carthaginians. The sally went terribly wrong, and Publius died fighting against dreadful odds, far from the force that he had left in the camp.

The Celtiberian's, meanwhile, had deserted Gnaeus, so he had begun a strategic retreat. However, he was not able to move fast enough. Hasdrubal Gisco's forces were joined by the jubilant armies of Mago and Hasdrubal Barca, who were all fired up and battle ready from their recent triumph over Publius. Gnaeus had his soldiers pile up the supply packs to make a rampart of sorts on a bare, rocky hill but they were soon overrun, and Gnaeus was killed.

The remnants of the army limped back across the Ebo under the guidance of Tiberius Fonteius, the commander Publius had left in charge at his camp, and under Lucius Marcius, a Roman knight from Gnaeus army. Although there were conflicting reports, it seems that

Lucius Marcius must have been an able commander for he continued to hold the front with possibly around 8000 infantry and about a thousand cavalry.

In 210, Rome decided to send reinforcements to Spain, but none of the senior generals were willing to undertake the endeavor. Apparently, they had had quite enough of breaking their hearts and their armies in Spain, against the Barcas. Besides, the war was going full tilt on the Sicilian front, and they had their hands full with Hannibal tearing up the countryside in the northern part of Italy.

But Publius Scipio had an axe to grind with the Barcas and the Carthaginians. Since his father and uncle had both lost their lives in Spain, he was hot for revenge. So he volunteered to make the journey into Spain.

Now, Aemilia would have a real reason to visit the temple daily, for Publius would be gone a long while, into an area that would be difficult, dangerous and – in the long run – very hard on his health. Although he would have, no doubt, have left a man of business in charge of his affairs, she would have been in charge of running the house in his absence. One has to wonder whether she was glad to be left in charge of things, or if she missed her husband during his many long absences. We have examples from literature to indicate how women were supposed to behave under these circumstances, but one has to wonder if she was a true Penelope, or if she were a more strong minded and independent.

Chapter 5: Carthago Nova and the Conquest of Spain

Have either accepted or jockeyed for the position, Scipio set out for Spain. There are conflicting accounts of the number of men and cavalry that he took with him, but the various writings indicate that his army was a mixture of Romans, levies from the provinces and – once he had arrived in Spain – the remnants of his uncle and father's armies. In any case, he was heavily outnumbered by the forces from Carthage.

As it happens, when Scipio first entered Spain, Hannibal was not there. In fact, Hannibal, having traveled over the Alps with his elephants and the rest of his army, was in Italy, making his way toward Rome. This might have been one reason that the older generals really were not interested in traveling to a foreign country to try to take more territory; they were intent in keeping the able Carthaginian commander off Rome's doorstep.

Under-manned as he was, Scipio decided to go for a soft target. Carthago Nova, or New Carthage had become the Barcas headquarters. It was situated on a peninsula that projected out into the sea, and was – the Barcas thought – only approachable from the land side. Because they believed that their fortifications were well established, Hannibal's younger brother, Hasdrubal, and brother Mago, had only left a small house-keeping force there, and had taken the rest of their army out in search of further conquests.

Considering that they had been channeling the wealth that they had been collecting from Spain through New Carthage, it was quite a plum – and ripe for the picking. Scipio must have smiled to think of the coup that he was about to pull off.

Scipio divided his forces, sending part of them with his friend and second in command, Laelius, to sail around on the seaward side and block the harbor. The rest of the troops he force-marched to the front side of the fortress, and – contrary to normal Roman custom – set up fortifications before establishing camp. Once he fortifications were up, he set up camp in the normal fashion, right out in front where the defenders could see him camped on their doorstep. Who knows how his ragtag mixed force viewed his actions, but the accounts available don't mention any rebellion or unhappiness about the target. Perhaps they appreciated the extra protection afforded by the fortifications.

At first, Scipio's army assaulted the front of the fortress – as the defenders probably expected. But he also talked with the local folk, and learned that at midday, the water was quite low on one side. Leaving part of his forces to continue the frontal assault, keeping the fighters who were manning the walls occupied, he took a small force around to the side of the keep, and scaled the undefended wall. With Laelius ready to hold off any chance of reinforcements from the sea, Scipio had New Carthage exactly where he wanted it – under his heel.

The subsequent carnage was said to be horrible. Scipio ordered his men to slay anyone in sight. They did a rampage through that fortress that would have done any barbarian horde proud, slaying, raping, pillaging. It might have partially been to strike terror to the hearts of the city's residents, but it might also have been in revenge for the deaths of the two older Scipios. When the dust had settled, Scipio rounded up the survivors. There were many youths and wives who had been held as hostages to ensure good behavior of native Spanish tribes. There were a few men who had been in charge; Scipio sent them back to Rome as hostages. And there were the ordinary folk – the shopkeepers, and artisans who were essential to keeping a city running. Scipio set the men of this latter group to work making weapons and engines of war with the understanding that after a time they would be set free.

Since he expected the Barcas to return to take back their city, Scipio kept his army well-trained and fit. He made them run with full packs, clean their weapons and themselves, and practice arms. But Carthage customarily executed military leaders who failed; so the Barcas were in no hurry to make their way back to Northern Africa. Therefore, for a whole year Scipio held New Carthage without so much as a whimper from the other armies.

Meanwhile, back in Rome and southern Italy, Hannibal was playing cat and mouse with the Roman forces. He didn't have enough men or supplies to actually take Rome, so he harried their forces. His hope was to wear them down to the point that they would not be able to defend their capital city. Instead, the older generals who were tired of war and wanted to be done with it, drove him slowly back until he was only occupying the toe of the Italian boot.

When Laelius brought back the prisoners to Rome from New Carthage, Scipio was hailed as a hero. However, it would be several months before Hannibal would learn that he had lost the city through which he and his brothers had been funneling the wealth of Spain as they acquired it.

Scipio took full advantage of the wealth stored in New Carthage. Among the hostages that he returned was a beautiful young woman who was betrothed to one of the local chieftains, along with the money her parents had paid for her ransom. The townfolk offered her to him as part of his booty, but with scarcely any consideration her turned down the offer, giving her into the keeping of her betrothed, untouched by his hands at least. Thus, the fellow became one of Scipio's loyal followers. Other chieftains also joined him. By returning the hostages to their families, Scipio began to win the loyalty of the local folk.

In addition to swelling the ranks of his troops with locals, Scipio also upgraded his soldiers gear. One of the changes he made was to issue double edged Spanish swords to his foot soldiers in place of the traditional Roman short sword, which was only sharp on one side.

In 209, Scipio took his troops and sallied forth to look for the three Carthaginian armies. He knew, however, that his armies were still vastly outnumbered, even though he had collected reinforcements from the Hispanic population. He did not want to get caught between the three forces from Carthage, so he found a time when Hasdrubal's army was separated from the other two. Scipio did a rare thing for him – he engaged in a traditional set battle – almost. While what seemed to be his total forces charged the center of Hasdrubal's forces, Scipio sneaked his reserves behind Hasdrubal's lines and attacked from the rear. This broke the back of the forces from Carthage, and allowed Scipio to win the battle – sending Hasdrubal limping away.

He declined, however, to pursue Hasdrubal's army. He received some criticism for this because Hasdrubal eventually made his way over the Alps in an effort to reinforce Hannibal's position. It was well known that Scipio's father and uncle had sacrificed their lives to keep Hasdrubal and Hannibal's other kin from bringing their armies over the Alps to serve as reinforcements for the able commander.

However, had Scipio chosen to pursue, it is very possible that his illustrious military career would have ended right there. In very short order after Hasdrubal's retreat, Mago and Gisco, the other two generals from Carthage moved their forces in to fill the gap. It is likely that had Scipio pursued Hasdrubal, he would have been trapped between the three armies.

At the Battle of Baecula, as Hasdrubal's defeat became known, Scipio captured a number of Hasdrubal's forces – among them a young Numidian lad. It turned out that the young Numidian was nephew to Masinissa, the prince who was in charge of the Numidian cavalry. Cannily, Scipio gave the boy a Roman costume, a cavalry unit to accompany him, and sent the boy to his uncle. This would prove to be significant later on.

It would be an error to portray Scipio as being the only Roman general opposing Hannibal and the other forces from Carthage. Marcellus and Crispinus were the consuls opposing Hannibal as he tried to force his way northward in Italy. Marcellus played cat and mouse with Hannibal for several seasons before he succeeded in driving Hannibal down into the toe of the Italian boot. Perhaps age was catching up with Marcellus – he was in his early sixties – or perhaps he was getting a lot of pressure from Rome to finish up already yet with this upstart from Africa. Whatever the reason, Marcellus rode with several of his senior officers to scout an area to ascertain its suitability as a battle staging ground.

Hannibal also had scouting parties in the area. As Marcellus and his party rode up a little hill that they had their eye on, Hannibal's cavalry surrounded the veteran general and killed him along with every man in his party. However, Crispinus got wind of what had happened, and quickly sent out messenger, letting people know that Marcellus had fallen. This was an important step because Marcellus was wearing his seal ring – the ring that he would use as a stamp to prove that orders sent under that seal were authentic. It was a canny move on Crispinus' part because Hannibal did, indeed, immediately send out false messages using Marcellus' ring. However, this move failed because Roman messengers managed to arrive ahead of the false orders. Crispinus, who had himself been recently gravely wounded, put Marcellus' second-in-command, Claudius Nero, in charge of the grieving troops. Nero was able to rally the men, and they fought on, giving Hannibal a very hard time.

Crispinus died of his wounds, so at the end of the season, the Roman senate had to make haste to elect two new consuls for the area that Marcellus and Crispinus had covered. The year was now 207 BC, and one of the consuls chosen was Claudius Nero. The other consul was Livius, who would be sent to Rimini. Nero's army was intended to merge with the legions under Praetor Fulvius to strengthen the southern front.

Hasdrubal, who had managed to make it over the Alps in better order than Hannibal had enjoyed after he made the trip, immediately began marching south through Gaul. The Gallic tribesmen had no desire to tangle with the army, and no real reason to back up Rome, so Hasdrubal marched along with little opposition. He wanted to let his brother know that help was on the way and to arrange for their armies to meet. He, therefore, sent a messenger who was well guarded on ahead to find Hannibal. In the message, Hasdrubal wrote out the route that he planned to take.

Roman scouts waylaid the messenger party, and captured the detailed message. When the soldiers saw that it was in Phoenician, they immediately took it to Nero. Nero quickly translated it, and then did something that could have gotten him tried for treason. Instead of following his orders and remaining in his assigned area, he left enough of his men with Fulvius to make it appear that the army was still at full strength. He, and 7,000 men slipped out of camp late at night, and force marched their way to join Livius and his forces. This was not as irresponsible as it might seem. Thanks to the captured missive, Nero knew that Hasdrubal had managed to add to his army as he marched along. Without Nero's reinforcements, Livius was likely to be in trouble.

Livius has set up fortifications along the bank of the Metauro River, where he could reasonably expect Hasdrubal to march, but without Nero's forces his army would not have been strong enough to prevail against Hasdrubal. By the time Nero joined him, Hasdrubal had an encampment on the opposite bank. Seeing the reinforcements joining Livius, Hasdrubal chose a slightly different route from the one he had originally planned, but one that would still take him south toward Hannibal's location. What he did not realize was that the road he had chosen would soon run along the base of some very large cliffs, placing his forces at extreme disadvantage.

Nero and Livius positioned their forces in such a way as to pin Hasdrubal against the cliffs. Then they set up a great cry, which panicked the elephants in the Carthaginian forces, causing them to run amok, trampling their own forces. Hasdrubal ordered the elephants put down, which their handlers did right away, but not before they created a great deal of damage.

Although Hasdrubal's forces put up a valiant fight, the Roman forces steadily pushed them back against the cliffs, allowing them no maneuvering room. They bore down upon them until, realizing that the end was at hand, Hasdrubal put on his best dress uniform and waded into the fray to die in a manner so as to make his country proud.

His gesture came to an anticlimactic ending, however. Nero and his 7,000 men quickly marched back to Fulvius, and slipped back into camp.

Fulvius was fighting against Hannibal, who had no idea what had happened until a bundle was lobbed into his camp. When it was opened, Hasdrubal's head was revealed. Hannibal had not seen his beloved younger brother for nearly ten years.

Hannibal is portrayed as being a soldier's soldier. He labored tirelessly to find new strategies, to use his troops wisely and to not sacrifice them in hopeless engagements. But Hasdrubal's death hit him hard.

Grieving, Hannibal retreated to Calabria, and stayed there for the rest of that year and the next. It was as if the fight had been knocked out of him and he had retreated to rest and to mourn.

Meanwhile, back in Spain, Scipio continued to harry the Carthaginians and to collect allies. Gisco and Mago also continued to swell the ranks of their armies. The Barcas gathered their forces at Ilipo – around seventy thousand foot soldiers, four thousand horsemen and thirty-two elephants. They settled on a plain that was large enough to accommodate them, in an area that would have been very near what is today the city of Seville. They had nearly twice the numbers that the Romans could muster.

Scipio did not immediately move to engage the army from Carthage. Instead, he traveled northward, then approached their encampment from upriver. As he worked his way down river toward them, Scipio collected reinforcements – many of them Iberian tribesmen who were grateful for the return of their kindred. Once there, he took up his position on a little hill that faced the hill where Gisco and Mago had their fortifications. But he still did not attack.

Instead, each morning he roused his troops, had them stand in formation and wait. The Carthaginian army did the same. Day after day, they held this session of standing in formation glaring at each other. As time went on, the army from Carthage got up later and later, until one morning they did not assemble at all. On that day, Scipio directed his soldiers to rest, to rise early the following day, to eat a hearty breakfast and to assemble on the battlefield at sunrise. No doubt his troops were beginning to wonder about this ritual, but they had seen how Publius Scipio worked, and they followed his commands.

When the sun came up, there was Scipio's army, ready to march on the forces assembled by Carthage. Gisco and Mago hastily roused their troops out of bed and sent them to the field without their breakfast. Thus, they came to the battlefield already disorganized and unready.

Battle of Ilipa

Having set up this incredible feint, Scipio was ready to take the Carthaginian Army. Some historians believe that this battle, rather than the later battle at Zama was Scipio's masterpiece of strategy.

Scipio had been doing more than just baiting the Carthaginians, however. He had been observing their formation, noticing that day after day, it never varied – even though the army he was facing was slower and slower to assemble. The Libyans, who seemed well trained, were given the center. Their Spanish allies were assembled in the wings, back by the cavalry and protected from the fore by the elephants.

We are not told how Scipio arranged his troops day by day. Perhaps he varied them, perhaps he selected a standard formation. But on the day of battle he certainly used a novel organization of his troops. He placed his Spanish troops in the center. While they were getting into position, the velites or skirmishers and the cavalry harassed the Carthaginian troops as they were assembling themselves. Unfed and ill prepared, the Carthaginians must have found that alone a terrifying experience. Scipio's battle hardened legionnaires took up positions on either flank. Not only did this present the Carthaginians a soft center to attack, it kept the Spanish troops from being able to defect at the last minute. No doubt Scipio remembered the troops that had deserted his uncle.

When the troops were truly in position, Scipio signaled the skirmishers and cavalry to withdraw to a position behind the legions. The Spaniards advanced – but very slowly, because Scipio had no intention of allowing these poorly trained troops to come into contact with the Libyans. The legions quick marched, a rank of them passing the slower moving Spaniards. Legionnaires and cavalry swung around to either end of the disgruntled Carthaginians, catching them in a pincher movement. At the same time, all of the Roman contingency let out a great shout, and continued to make noise. This alarmed the elephants, causing them to run back through their own troops.

This placed the Libyans in a quandary. If they turned to face the forces coming up on their flanks they would present a vulnerable flank to the advancing Spaniards. Meanwhile the rampaging elephants were creating havoc. The Romans had the Carthaginians in an unenviable position. The situation looked grim for them.

Just then, the heavens opened up, and there was a torrential downpour. Drenched to the skin, the Roman forces retreated from the forces of mother nature. Without this natural intercession, the Carthaginians would have been in a bad way. As it was, they were able to also retreat, fleeing the scene of battle.

Thus, in 206, Scipio completely won Spain for the Roman Empire. This final battle sent the Carthaginians scurrying away for less contentious targets. In the case of Hasdrubal, the retreat took him over the Alps to attempt to join his brother, Hannibal.

Mutiny in the Ranks

However, Scipio's victory was not without cost. He fell ill after Ilipa, and had a rough time recovering. Perhaps it was the wetting they received, perhaps it was the many months in the field. Rumors of his demise ran through the ranks of the Roman army and its allies.

Many of his soldiers had grown resentful of their long, hard battles. Many of them were owed quite a lot of back pay, since Rome had not been very forthcoming with finances, replacement troops or supplies. They were tired of field rations, camping out and combat. At Sucro, they decided to mutiny. The mutineers included some of the native tribes, who felt that they had not received appropriate credit for their part in the victory at Ilipa. The mutineers pretended to honor the leaders of their cohorts, but instead replaced them with their own ringleaders. The men who refused to join the mutiny slipped away to join the troops that were located at New Carthage – which was, incidentally, the area where Scipio was convalescing.

There were 7000 loyal troops and 8000 mutineers. Rather than have a pitched battle between his own men, Scipio chose what seemed to be a diplomatic approach. He sent the seven loyal tribunes who had been driven out by the mutineers to talk with them about their grievances and to reassure them that Scipio was very much alive and in good health.

They seemed to come to an understanding. The native tribes that had participated in the mutiny withdrew to their own camps, and refrained from any additional rebellion. Scipio held a huge feast for the ringleaders of the mutineers, and when they were thoroughly drunk, he had his loyal tribunes arrest them. The mutinous troops were gathered in the square to witness the trial of these men, and then scolded for their participation in the mutiny. Most of the fight went out of them when the ringleaders were lashed, and then beheaded.

All of the troops were then given their back pay; and the mutineers had to make new vows of allegiance.

In 205, Scipio gave up the generalship in Spain, and returned to Rome. There, he held games in celebration; not for having conquered Spain, but for having put down the rebellion. It is said that he flung himself into these games with abandon, putting all of his grief, anger and frustration into the way he threw javelins and entered into competitions.

Chapter 6: Consul Scipio

After his return in 205, Publius Scipio was elected consul. With this official endorsement in hand, he planned to take his army to Africa, to bring the conflict to Carthage. However, he was only thirty years old, and the minimum age for consul was forty. Therefore, his detractors conspired to limit his troop strength by limiting his budget and saying that he could only take volunteers. However, many of the men who had fought with him in Spain were loyal, and he was able to raise additional troops, including veterans of the Battle of Cannae. More than that, many of the wealthy citizens of Rome and Italy recognized him as an able commander, and quickly began to make contributions to his campaign – ships, grain, pig iron – which helped relieve his slender purse.

As he marched his army toward Sicily, Publius Scipio was able to take Locri Epizephyrii, a city located in the very toe of Italy – one that had been traded back and forth between the Romans and their enemies for many centuries. At the time, it was an harbor that frequently welcomed Carthaginian ships. By conquering it, Scipio cut off a major source of supplies for Hannibal. Having struck a small blow against Hannibal, Scipio sailed to Sicily.

Sicily became his training ground, and the area where men and goods continued to pour in to assist Scipio with his ambitious effort to take the war to Carthage instead of waiting for it to come to him. Now, an interesting thing about his becoming the consul of Sicily: it also made him de facto governor of Sicily. For some time, the island had been a punishment station for soldiers who "failed" in other areas. Two legions were veterans of both Cannae and of Marcellus army. They were hardened veterans who were just as eager as the young commander to have done with Carthage, the Barcas and Hannibal Barca in particular.

In addition to these troops, Scipio gained troops from the Sicilians themselves. As a province of Rome, they were exempt from contributing men to the army. However, they could not own their land, and they had to pay taxes to Rome. In exchange, Rome was to provide military protection. Scipio found some sort of loophole in Roman law which allowed him to return lands to Sicilian control. In exchange, the grateful recipients provided militia at their own expense. He also gained Sicily as a loyal supply base for his troops.

Knowing very well that venturing into Africa where he had no supply base was risky business, and knowing that his new army was an amazing mixture of veterans with a variety of background and green, new troops who had never been in a battle, as well as contributions from the tribes in Spain where he had won some loyalty and respect, he began two processes. On the one hand, he began putting his men through extreme training sessions. On the other, he spent his nights visiting campfires, listening to stories and learning about the region. Since Sicily was so close to North Africa, the natives had considerable knowledge of the area.

In addition, he sent Laelius, his friend and second-in-command, with a fleet of ships to scout along the coast of North Africa. Scipio also asked Laelius to contact Syphax and Masinissa, and to sound them out on the possibility of joining with them in opposition to Carthage. Syphax and Masinissa were both rulers in Numidia, the source of the fearsome Numidian cavalry that had been such as asset to Hamilcar.

It was while he was busy gathering intelligence and training his men, it came to Scipio's ears that the port of Locri was about to defect from Carthaginian rule back to Rome. Scipio quickly lead a troop of three thousand soldiers into Locri, securing it for Rome.

Locri is located on the eastern side of the toe of the Italian boot. It is part of the Calabrian area where Hannibal had taken refuge after his brother, Hasdrubal's death. Calabria is an ideal region for an army to lose itself, and a difficult area from which to extract it once it has dug in. Even to this day, it is a rocky, mountainous region. When one thinks of Italy, sunny beaches, slopes with grape vines and warmth come to mind. But the plateau in that area is high enough to have snow and evergreens. The area is rugged, and even has some active volcanic activity. It was into this inhospitable region that Hannibal had entrenched himself.

In spite of his success in securing Locri, Scipio came under censure for his actions. He had moved his troops out of his assigned area, and encroached on territory belonging to another commander. The Senate sent out a team to investigate and to question Scipio about his motives in this move. However, their criticism was muted by the simple fact that Licinius, the consul who was supposed to be over that area, had done very little to slow or contain Hannibal.

Scipio had reduced the size of the cage for the Lion of Carthage.

In the spring of 204 BC, Scipio was made proconsul over the area. He loaded his entire army onto a fleet of forty warships and four hundred transport ships. He had 26,000 soldiers, forty-five days' worth of food and water, of which fifteen days' worth were pre-cooked. It normally took a day and a night to sail from Sicily to northern Africa, but if the winds were unfavorable it might take longer.

They had intended to land on a cape west of Carthage, but instead found themselves on a cape to the east. This meant that in order to reach their intended destination, they had to sail around the Bay of Tunis. Carthage lay inside that bay!

There was no response from Carthage, however, and Scipio successfully landed his army near Utica, the second largest city in Carthage's territory.

The news upon landing was not good. Upon his father's death, Syphax had taken over Numidia, and had firmly sided with Carthage. Carthage had offered him alliance and Gisco's daughter's hand in marriage to seal the deal. She was formerly to have married Masinissa, but apparently Carthage found Syphax to be the better bet. Although Numidia had formerly been two allied kingdoms, it was now only one.

Masinissa brought a mere two hundred horsemen. But he brought something else: friendship. Apart from the loyal Laelius, Scipio had few that he could call friend. He welcomed Masinissa, against whom he had fought, and recognized in him a military strategist who could mesh with his current commanders. The three men were all in their early thirties, all career military, and all dedicated to acting honorably in battle. These were characteristics that would set them apart from Hannibal, who had only his brothers upon whom to rely.

Carthage responded oddly to Utica being under siege, leaving Scipio's army little to do beyond looting and pillaging the surrounding countryside. Part of this was because the Carthaginians were unused to war at home, and it took them a while to put together a force of mercenaries and Syphax' cavalry with which to respond. This was made more difficult for them in that the previous year, 205 BC, they had sent Mago, Hannibal's youngest brother, to Genoa in an effort to get men and supplies around the Roman naval blockade.

As a result, Rome took little notice of Scipio's slow progress. They sent a consul and two praetors with six legions to meet Mago as he entered Italy from over the Alps. Unlike when Hannibal had created a route at Cannae, the Gauls did not join Mago's army. Apparently, they saw that Rome was prevailing against Carthage, and they had no desire to join the losing side. Consequently, even though the military men sent against Mago were of ordinary caliber, they sent

Hannibal's little brother back to Genoa to lick his wounds. At the same time, although Hannibal did not retreat any farther than Calabria, neither did he manage to advance.

Battle of Utica

The older Romans had believed in battle with honor, and winning straight out, without subterfuge or trickery. But Hannibal had taught the young commanders of Scipio's generation another lesson: war is not fair, and a win by trickery is still a win.

Near Scipio's winter camp was the Carthaginian/Numidian camp. Traditionally, war was not carried out in winter. When spring would arrive, so would combat. Scipio suggested to Syphax that further combat was not in either of their best interest, and perhaps Syphax would like to be the go-between who would broker a peace agreement between Rome and Carthage. Syphax had what he wanted out of the current conflict. He was the ruler of Numidia, he had a beautiful young wife, and it seemed to him that negotiating peace between these two leading powers would be just the thing to make his reputation complete.

Scipio began sending an envoy with a retinue back and forth between the camps. The envoy seemed to be a harmless, elderly patrician who was accompanied by his slaves and servants. In actual fact, his retinue was a coterie of seasoned soldiers who took the opportunity at each negotiation to collect information about the Carthaginian/Numidian camp. It is truly amazing how much information a slave or nosy servant can glean from an area. The peace talks were a ruse designed solely to collect information. Scipio knew very well that Rome would not accept any peace treaty; they had lost too much to Hannibal's depredations, and they wanted revenge more than peace. But he was not about to tell Syphax that. Instead, he bided his time while he built up data about the enemy encampment.

When Scipio had gathered all the intelligence he felt he needed, spring was approaching. The envoy made one last trip to tell Syphax, regretfully, that Rome had decided to break off negotiations. He then gave the appearance of resuming the siege of Utica.

However, only a third of the army laid siege. The other two-thirds were prepared for a night raid on the other army's camp. This plan was so secret that even the generals in charge of the troops were not told of the plan until the night it was to take place. Scipio told only his most trusted commanders.

It was agreed that Masinissa and Laelius would attack the Numidian encampment first. Their shelters were made of wood and reeds, and would burn easily. Scipio would take the other third of their forces and attack the Carthaginians as soon as he saw the flames going up from the Numidian encampment.

The two parties left the Roman encampment around 9:00 pm, or just at the end of First Watch. For the next two watches, they marched toward their chosen destinations. Masinissa and Laelius arrived at the Numidian camp around three o'clock am – just at the end of third watch. They shot fire arrows into the reed huts of the Numidian's who rushed out, thinking that the fire had been set accidentally. When they realized that they were under attack, it was too late to dash back for their weapons that were inside the now blazing huts. In the panic, nearly as many men were crushed by their terrified comrades as were killed by the Roman soldiers. Many accounts estimate that there were sixty thousand soldiers in Syphax' camp.

The Carthaginians also believed that it must be an accidental fire. They climbed to the top of the walls in their camp to view what was going on. Now, however, fire arrows came raining into their camp, as well. Within moments, the same scenario was enacted in the Carthaginian camp.

Gisco and Syphax managed to escape the carnage, each with a handful of soldiers. Gisco returned to Carthage, and Syphax fled to Numidia. Many of the soldiers, who were mercenaries if you will recall, simply scattered into the bush to escape the swords and spears of the night raiders. Scipio did not attempt to catch any of them. He had accomplished his goal. The army was demoralized, and war had been tacitly declared.

Battle of the Plains

It did not take Carthage long to recover, however. Many of the scattered soldiers slipped back into the city to rejoin their units. Gisco's daughter, Syphax' new wife, pleaded with him and he agreed to back Carthage once again. Both armies were somewhat reduced by the night raid, so the effort was not completely wasted.

Gisco marched his Carthaginian army toward the Numidian capital city to add a little more pressure to his daughter's pleading with her husband. The Carthaginians needed that able Numidian cavalry to help prevail against Scipio. The plan was to meld the two armies outside the city, and then to march against the Roman forces. Scipio learned of their plan, and decided to send his own army to this meeting.

Masinissa and Laelius lead the fighting force that crashed Gisco and Syphax's party, so to speak. When they came to the field, they found that they were facing not only the remnants of the forces that had escaped the night raid, they were also facing 4,000 fresh mercenary troops from Iberia. In spite of the reinforcements, they won the battle, and bound Syphax in chains, preparatory to sending him to Rome. His wife, Sophonisbe, met Masinissa at the gates. She declared her undying love, and upon seeing the woman who had once been his betrothed, Masinissa did not hesitate. He married her, and thus regained his kingdom.

However, when Scipio heard about it, he was not pleased with his friend's nuptials. It is possible that he feared for the man's life; or it could have been that he feared Sophonisbe's powers of persuasion – she had already fed one man to her father's war machine, after all. Or it could simply have been that Scipio was, indeed, following the rules for dealing with the enemies of Rome. Whatever the reason, he explained that she would have to be sent to Rome as part of the spoils of war.

When he heard that, Masinissa sent to Sophonisbe a letter explaining the situation, and a vial of poison. The letter stated that it was a husband's duty to protect his wife, and if he could not do that, to spare her from unbearable suffering. Apparently, she found being sent to Rome a fate worse than death, so she took the poison. Her last words were, "I accept this wedding gift from my husband."

Needless to say, this whole thing was upsetting to Masinissa, and Scipio could see that his friend was in the depths of sorrow. In an effort to cheer him up, Scipio assembled the entire army and had them witness his congratulations to Masinissa. He then declared him to be a friend to Rome, and an ally. He presented Masinissa with a scarlet war-tent. These were usually reserved for the Roman consuls, so this was an honor, indeed.

Syphax was escorted to Rome and placed under a sort of permanent house arrest. Ironically, he remained there for the rest of his life, living quietly in a state of reasonable health, and eventually dying of natural causes. Had Sophonisbe gone with him, it is possible that she, also, might have survived. One must wonder what might have been her state of mind upon receiving a vial of poison from her newest husband. One also must wonder how sincere were Masinissa's protestations of love if a scarlet tent and military honors were sufficient to comfort him.

The Roman senate approved Scipio's actions, welcoming Masinissa as their first ally in Africa. As for Masinissa, who can say – looking through the glass of time darkly – what were his real reactions. It all seems a bit surreal and more than a little over the top.

The governing body of Carthage was in extreme disarray. This was the first time that they had lost a battle on their own soil. Various factions each had their own pet solution for the situation. In the end, they implemented four proposals. They mobilized their navy to attack Roman ships, and they set about fortifying the walls around Carthage. Envoys with official papers were immediately sent to Rome to recall Hannibal and Mago. Another envoy was sent to Scipio to suggest that they open negotiations for peace.

Scipio responded with genuine interest to the peace treaty. Just to show how earnest were his efforts to actually bring about peace, here is a list of his proposals:

- Rome would recognize Carthage as an independent nation, and it would remain autonomous

- All Carthaginian armies would withdraw from Italy and from Gaul
- Carthage would renounce all interest in Spain
- Carthage would recognize Masinissa as king of Numidia
- Carthage would surrender all but twenty of its warships to Rome
- Carthage would supply the Roman army in Africa during negotiations
- Carthage would pay five thousand talents (about fifty million dollars in today's economy) in war reparations

However, it soon became clear that those negotiations were primarily to allow Hannibal time to bring his veteran forces back from Italy in order to oppose Scipio's armies. As Hannibal was returning, he captured a Roman supply fleet that had run aground. When Rome sent envoys to protest this violation of the peace treaty, the envoys were killed. Perhaps this was a statement or retaliation to Scipio's devious plan that lead to burning the Carthaginian winter camp. Either way, it is likely that Hannibal found the supplies useful.

It is written in some accounts that Hannibal had so few ships in which he could transport his army from the toe of the Italian boot that he shoved soldiers away from the ships as he was leaving. What could have been in the hearts and minds of those men as they were left on the shores of Italy with no viable way home?

In all events, this the capture of the supply fleet reopened the conflict. It would culminate in the battle fought just outside Zama, the Numidian capital.

Chapter 7: The Battle of Zama

In 202, Publius Africanis and Hannibal Barca arrayed their armies on the plains of Zama in north Africa. It must have been an amazing sight: two great armies spread out before each other. Scipio had his infantry organized in columns, with skirmishers filling in the gaps in between. On one flank, he had his seasoned Italian cavalry; on the other, he had Masinissa's Numidian cavalry – a formidable force that had formerly fought with Hannibal in Spain, but were now, thanks to the recent victory over Syphax, allied with Rome. It is interesting that Numidia vacillated between being allied with Carthage and allied with Rome, and that each change of side influenced the course of a battle.

Hannibal had drawn up his armies in three ranks. He placed his barbarian mercenaries in the front ranks, then a row of less experienced fighters, then finally his seasoned troops at the back. This was not entirely unlike

Scipio's tactics at Ilipa. Had Hannibal been studying his young rival's methods? Certainly, Scipio had been studying his, and learning the lessons taught very well.

Hannibal's elephants were near the front of the army, where they were less likely to trample their own people. The plan was to wear down the Romans with the elephants and barbarians, then the veterans would be able to mop up the remains.

As it happens, Scipio had the accounts of former battles with elephants, as well as some experience. He knew that allowing them to run amok among his foot soldiers would end the battle before it began; but he also knew that properly managed, those elephants could become a two-edge sword, a weapon that could be turned against the wielder. He planned to take advantage of their temperamental natures.

The skirmishers were instructed to specifically target the elephants and their handlers, encouraging them to run down the aisles Scipio had conveniently created between the regular foot soldiers' formations. The skirmishers would melt away into the regular formations, leaving clear aisles for the elephants to run through. As the elephants pursued their tormentors, the soldiers were instructed to blow on brass horns, to beat their spears on their shields and to yell loudly. They also threw javelins at the elephants and their handlers. The massed noise was too much even for these battle-trained beasts. Many of them simply ran down the corridors provided. A few bolted through the formations, but many of them – particularly those whose handlers had been slain -- turned around, charging into the ranks of Hannibal's massed troops, creating considerable carnage.

Faced with a ferocious foe and raging elephants, the mercenary troops in the center of Hannibal's formation turned to flee, only to be met with the spears and swords of Hannibal's regulars. Given a choice between being skewered by their own side or fighting Scipio's troops, they turned and fought.

Meanwhile, Scipio's cavalry had routed Hannibal's cavalry, and had given chase instead of sticking with the battle – something that probably irritated the able commander. However, they returned in the nick of time, swooping down on the flanks of the carnage occurring on the battlefield. Hannibal's veterans were brave – and were probably very much aware of the Carthaginian practice of executing failed soldiery – but they were unable to win out against Scipio's tactics.

Had not the Numidian cavalry and Scipio's regular cavalry rejoined Scipio's army, the outcome might have been very different. But the added veteran horse soldiers, along with Scipio's tactics, won the day.

There is some speculation that the Battle of Zama is a fiction created by the Romans to counter-balance their horrific defeat at Canae. There is no marker for the battle field, no dig has turned up weapons or bones. But it should be remembered that the plains of Africa are vast – even near Carthage. And local people have a way of picking up the remains of war and using them for themselves. Perhaps the battle was exaggerated – finding exact numbers for troops is difficult from this end of time's telescope. But it is probable that some such battle took place. It is known for certain that it was within this time frame that Rome broke Phoenician dominance of the Mediterranean.

The carnage at Zama was devastating, and it was nearly the last straw for Carthaginian rule. Hannibal managed to escape, leading a small force back to Hadrumetum. From there, he recommended that Carthage accept Rome's terms for peace. Hannibal would then become the acting ruler of Carthage, and would conduct an investigation into the handling of accounts while Hamilcar, his brother, and his sons were in Spain and in Italy, and generally point fingers at the nobles of that city. They would then turn the tables on him, and accuse him of treason, forcing Hannibal to flee. But that is an account for a different chapter.

Chapter 8: Triumphus Scipio Africanus

In 201, Publius Scipio, now Africanus, returned a hero. As he and his troops marched back into Rome, they were showered with flowers. Publius received official honors, and a statue that was robed in fine clothing and crowned with laurel leaves. But more than the victory earned in Africa, the Roman people were celebrating a return to peace. They were tired of war – which had been going on for more than 16 years. Far too much of the fighting had taken place in Italy. They were truly ready for peace, and they hailed Publius Scipio Africanis as the instrument of having ended all of the fighting.

Scipio would have some time to spend with his wife and his children. In 199, he was censor and become Princeps Senatus, or the head of the senate. But he was not without detractors. While Scipio had been in Spain, garnering victories and pushing back the Barcas, other generals had been battling directly against

Hannibal on Italian soil. It is likely that they were jealous of his honors and more than a little bit tired of the upstart young commander.

Scipio's high-handed and individualistic ways of achieving his victories had caused a certain amount of rancor among the other military commanders – particularly those who territories had been encroached. More than that, Scipio, whose health had never been stellar, was not a well man. His health, after all, had been part of the mutiny that had occurred in Spain because the troops had feared that they were losing their able commander.

Greece was now the nation where unrest was rearing its head. During the conflict with Carthage – what the Romans of the day called "Hannibal's War" and history would term the second Punic War – most of Greece had lent its support to Rome. The exception was Macedonia, which had allied itself with Hannibal.

It should be understood that the princeps senatus was not a ruler or the head of the senate in the way that a king might have ruled or even the way the President of the United States or the way the Prime Minister of Great Britain might function. In fact, the closest modern equivalent might be the Speaker of the House in the United States modern government. The princeps had some power, but it was mostly manifested by the privilege to speak first in meetings.

After the reign of Alexander the Great, which had ended in 323 BC, skirmishes among the city states and the three regions given to Alexander's generals had been common.

One of the first moves by the Roman senate after Scipio's triumphant return was to dispatch diplomatic messengers to these regions in an effort to maintain diplomatic peace. One of these went to Egypt, where sending thanks for Egypt's continued neutrality in the recent conflict. Another went to Philip of Macedonia, deploring recent aggression against Athens, and suing for a peaceful resolution to differences.

The messenger to Macedonia was a little late, however. Macedonian troops were already on the march, headed toward Athens. The Senate agreed that the Macedonians needed to be stopped, and that they should be taught a lesson. But the Citizens' Assembly voted against sending any military against Macedonia. They had only recently been able to enjoy the benefits of peace and they had no desire to send more young men into battle.

Galba, who had been recently elected consul, appealed to the Roman people. He noted that if assistance had been sent to Publius Scipio – the one who was killed in Spain, along with his brother Gnaeus – that the recent war would have been fought in Spain rather than in Rome. He argued that the recent conflict with Hannibal had started in much the same way as the moves that Phillip of Macedonia was making – taking one or two little towns that are not much noticed, then one or two more, until those little military victories became large victories. And when those victories became large enough, they had resulted in Hannibal crossing the Alps, a direction from which Rome had not expected any problems, and bringing the fight to Italy through the Gallish states. Galba pointed out that diplomacy had not worked at Sagunto. He also pointed out that if Philip took Athens, then next was probably Corinth, and that Corinth was only five days away from Rome when traveling by sea.

After Galba's speech, the Citizens' Assembly endorsed a declaration of war against Macedonia. However, the army that was sent, they said, must be made up of volunteers.

Knowledge of the chance of intervention was enough to cause Philip to pull his army back from Athens. Instead, he focused on Pergamon and Rhodes. However, this did not in any major way reduce the threat. Alliances and non-alliances were constantly being forged and broken. Some of these were made through marriages – particularly between Syria, Pergamon and Egypt. Still, in spite of the occasional domestic spat, relations between these regions had remained relatively calm. Furthermore, Rome tended to honor her agreements with those within her circle of influence, her hegemony, by extending the protection of her armies.

This might be a good time to talk about the word hegemony. It is a relatively modern word which refers to the influence of power. It is nothing so crass as colonization, but it certainly implies influence. By creating diplomatic connections with surrounding nations, Rome extended her hegemony. This buffer of positive influence protected the central core region of Italy from external invasion. It did not exclude Rome from the general turbulence that resulted from local political and military maneuvering.

In Macedonia Greeks were under uneasy rule by outsiders. Sparta and Athens, both major players in political ebb and flow between city states rarely presented a unified front. They saw the rising national star, Rome, as being a way to teach the Macedonians a lesson and to get out from under their rule.

Rome, however, had no desire to confront Macedonia to such extent. Bloody their collective noses and keep them off the Roman doorstep, to be sure, but they had no real need to conquer territory in that direction. Furthermore, Rome had a deep admiration of all things Greek, particularly art works and literature. This admiration somewhat hampered their ability to see Greece in the same light as other nations that existed to be conquered. Scipio and Flaminius, both of whom were highly influential in the conflict against Macedonia, Flaminius, in particular, saw himself as a liberator destined to free the Greek city-states from the tyrannical Macedonians.

Even with a declaration of war, it was three years before an army made up of Roman volunteers and Greeks confronted the Macedonian forces at Cynoscephalae in Thessaly. Approximately 10,000 of the troops were Roman, and the other 10,000 Greek. Macedonia had 26,000 men. Flaminius, who was in charge of this force, had made extensive study of Scipio's methods – which had, in turn, been learned by studying Hannibal's exceptionally effective strategies.

In spite of having superior forces, the Macedonian's lost the battle. The Romans lost only 700 men, while 5,000 of the Macedonians were taken prisoner. King Philip requested time to bury his dead and to sue for peace.

The Greek city states of the Aetolian League objected to this leniency. They argued that if they invaded now, they could defeat Philip V once and for all. However, Rome had no particular desire to conquer Macedonia – merely to stop Philip V from potential invasion. They explained gently to the Greeks that it was Roman policy to be magnanimous to their opponents.

They also pointed out that Macedonia provided a buffer between Greece and the Celts and Thracians to the north. Flaminius went on to suggest that the Greeks find a way to peacefully coexist with Macedonia to their mutual benefit.

Subsequently a peace treaty was signed with Macedonia that limited the size of its army, returned all the Greek cities within its control to their own recognizance, and remanded other territories not originally part of Macedonia to Roman rule, and required Macedonia to pay one thousand talents to Rome by way of reparation – 500 of which were to be paid immediately, and the remainder to be paid in installments over the next ten years.

The Grecian communities were now safe. The Macedonians had ceased their aggression; but the Greeks were still worried. What if Rome decided to take them over? At the Corinthian games that year, the commander Titus Quinctius Flaminius made an announcement that set their minds at rest. He decreed that Greece was completely free of Roman rule, owing no taxes or tribute to Rome. Greece would be entirely self-governing, subject only to its own rule. Flaminius even asked the Greeks to track down the Roman soldiers that Hannibal had captured twenty years before, at the battle of Cannae, and return those veterans to Rome.

However, even though Scipio maintained a vigorously pro-Hellenic policy, he argued against withdrawing all troops from Greece. While he heartily endorsed the idea of Roman hegemony, and he had great admiration for anything Greek, he was also a realist. He knew that peace was only likely to be upheld if all members of treaties and agreements endorsed it. Although Syria and Egypt had not joined the general fray, that did not mean that they were completely acquiescent.

When he was again elected consul again in 194, he continued to argue against military withdrawal, fearing that Antiochus, the king of

Syria, would invade. In 193, his fears proved to be correct.

Meanwhile, Hannibal had chosen to tighten the belts of the Carthaginian nobles rather than raise taxes in order to defray Carthage's war expenses. Consequently, some of those unhappy nobles complained to Rome, and Rome sent someone to inspect the conquered city. Hannibal, anticipating that this was unlikely to mean anything good for him, boarded a ship before the inspecting party could arrive, and sailed away to join Antiochus in Syria.

In 190, Scipio served as legate for his brother Lucius. Together, they sailed to Asia. At Magnesia, Lucius won a victory over Antiochus, gaining the name Asiagenus. Publius, however, was too ill to take part in the battle. Yet, it was thanks to this battle that Hannibal, who had fled to the court of Antiochus, drank poison rather than fall into the hands of the Romans.

Scipio and his brother Lucius had not risen to power without making a certain number of enemies. Scipio had a reputation for being an exceptional orator, able to sway troops to follow him into impossible battles and to gain their trust and loyalty. However, sometimes in the course of persuading people, Scipio could depart from strictest truth.

When he was gaining the loyalty of troops in Spain, he made some fairly outrageous claims – just by way of example. He stated that Poseidon was his real father, and that his strength and abilities were beyond those of mortal man. Apparently, even though his father was dead and beyond disputing his claims, Scipio had no problem at all suggesting that his mother had sexual congress with a god. After all, it at least put her in good company, although those ladies from mythology who dallied with deities rarely came to a good end.

Could it possibly be that the golden-tongued orator told one too many whoppers in his efforts to sway the masses? Or had he simply stepped on too many toes in headlong rush to various positions of authority, gaining them in spite of the senate, completely ignoring their protests. Perhaps his easy way with his soldiers, gaining their loyalty and admiration, made certain others nervous.

Whatever the reason, by the time of Lucius's Asian campaign, Scipio Africanis the Elder had no few detractors in the Senate. More than that, it is entirely possible that his own children were a source of disappointment to him. Scipio Africanis the younger was frail of health and could not hold office, two of his youngsters were girls, and his other son seems to have been a fairly ordinary sort of fellow.

Still, his twilight years were not without their bright spots. Scipio Africanis the Younger became an augur – one of the priest class who were responsible for reading the signs and portents that would indicate the likelihood of success or failure of a venture. Augury was important to the Romans of that time, and scarcely any venture could be undertaken without reading the signs of the times. Furthermore, unlike appointments to more secular offices, an appointment as augur was for life. This younger Scipio would eventually adopt Scipio Amelius, a young man who would play a significant role in the third Punic war. But more of that later.

Chapter 9: Ungrateful Fatherland, You Shall not have my bones

In Scipio's later years, all did not go well for the Cornelii brothers. Lucius was accused of not reporting or accounting for 500 talents received from Antiochus, this was in 187. In 184, Africanis was also accused. Whether the brothers had been victims of fraud and false accusations or whether Lucius – as some accounts speculate – had used the funds to support the army, the repercussions were upsetting and devastating to both brothers.

Angry, upset, accused of bribery and treason, Scipio withdrew to a villa he owned near Liturnum in Campania. There, he tilled the land with his own hands, living very quietly and simply. A friend remarked upon how straitened were his circumstance – for example, he commented on how small and cold was the bathroom when compared to the more spacious chamber that had been in Scipio's house in

Rome. Accounts do not say what Aemilia thought of the move. It is unlikely that she was given any say in the matter. However, it was suggested in some accounts that Scipio's withdrawal was not entirely without comfort, and that he made use of the companionship of one of the household's women. The point was made that thanks to Papiria's divorce, and having seen first hand what happens to divorced women, that Aemilia simply looked the other way while Scipio carried out his affair.

It is also said that Scipio was so angry with Rome for the perfidy of the other senators that he directed that he should be buried in Liturnum rather than in the ancestral Cornelii tomb in Rome. He is believed to have requested the following inscription on his grave marker, "Ungrateful fatherland, you shall not have my bones." However, the location and the marker have long since been lost.

At age fifty-three, he passed away on his small estate. And he was, indeed, buried there rather than in Rome. A contemporary, describing the grave marker, said that it was very like an altar, and that Scipio's comment on his homeland was engraved on its side.

Some historians are of the opinion that it was about this time that the flavor of Rome began to change. As a society, Rome was always a "work in progress." During the course of its history (up until that time) it had moved from a primarily agrarian society that was patriarchally governed to a Republic that offered opportunity to freedmen and common folk as well as to the nobility. It even offered a slender hope for slaves to free themselves and to even become citizens.

The Senate had, these folk say, become corrupt. Many of the ruling class were, once again, more focused on what they could gain than what they could give. They felt that it was no wonder that Scipio had withdrawn from Roman society in disgust.

Yet his influence was not completely lacking, for he left several descendants who continued to carry out the Cornelius name and who had felt the old man's influence. While most of them were fairly ordinary, his adopted grandson grew to be remarkably similar in his battle prowess and his tendency to innovate. Even the descendants who were children of his daughters had their time and their influence. The old man's adherence to principle and his ability to step on influential toes continued to come out in the younger generations.

As the Roman Empire continued to spread itself wide around the Mediterranean and beyond, as it developed Emperors, alliances and enemies, the seed of Scipio Africanus continued to have influence for about four generations before the line seemed to quietly dwindle away.

Modern architects have speculated that there might have been several reasons for some of the older patrician families to have slowly died out. Cities in that time were notoriously unclean, and without adequate sanitation they would have been hotbeds of disease. In addition to that, the

Roman love of indoor plumbing might have also had an influence. Lead, which was malleable and easy to form was often used to make the pipes that carried water. It has been suggested that this lead to such aberrations as the Nero who is said to have played a musical instrument while Rome burned around him. Although, in all fairness to the water of the time, it has also been suggested that calcification from the water would soon have coated the inside of the pipes, mitigating the effects of the lead that was used to make the pipes.

Lead was also used in such things as the seals for bottles of wine. Wine was considered to be a refined drink – and with all of its rocky hillsides, Rome was an excellent location for vineyards.

Chapter 10: Descendants of Publius Scipio Africanus the Elder

Sometime around 216, Publius Scipio Cornelius Africanis had married Aemilia, the third daughter of Amelius Paulus – as previously mentioned. Amelius Paulus had been one of the consuls who fell at Cannae. Scipio and Aemilia Tertia had four children: Publius Scipio Africanis the younger, who was barred from public service because of ill health, and so became an augur; Cornelia Scipio Major (daughter); Lucius Cornelius Scipio (second son); and (?); Cornelia Africana Scipio Minor b. 190.

Publius Scipio Africanis the younger was elected augur, thus becoming a priest of sorts – even though he did not campaign for office. He adopted the second son of Lucius Amelius Paulus Macedonicus, as he did not have any children of his own in an effort to maintain the Corneli line. Now, here is where we prove that the modern world is not alone is following the lives of the rich and famous. Lucius Aemilius Paulus Macedonicus divorced his wife, Papiria Madonis. Lucius was son to the same Aemilius who was the consul who died at Cannae, and was also brother to Scipio Africanus' wife. Lucius and Papiria had four children at the time, two boys and two girls. As was the custom of the times, the children remained with their father. He remarried, and had two more boys. Since it was expensive to foster boys through the cursus honorium or the succession of offices expected of patrician sons, he adopted out the older two boys when they were ages 14 and 9. The elder was adopted by Quintus Fabius Maximus, thus becoming Quintus Fabius Maximus Aemillius; the younger was adopted by his cousin Scipio Africanus the Younger, becoming Publius Cornelius Scipio Aemillius – a young man whose military genius somewhat resembled that of his adoptive grandfather. Scipio Aemillius would make his mark in the third Punic war, and would earn the name of Scipio Africanus the Younger.

Without a husband, and having been divorced, Papiria's fate was pitiable. She spent the several years living in poverty. Perhaps it was her fate, in part, that influenced Scipio Africanis the Younger to adopt his cousin. In addition, it might very well have influenced his mother to look the other way when Scipio Africanis the Elder was rumored to have an affair with one of the household females. Clearly, Aemilia, wife of Scipio Africanis the Elder, enjoyed the wealth and influence brought to her by her marriage. She also had four children to consider; and she, in all probability, did not wish to suffer Papiria's fate. Even the straitened circumstance to which the family was reduced when living at the country villa would have been preferable.

However, Papiria survived to get the last laugh on the second wife. When her ex-husband died, his estate went to his older two sons. Scipio divided his portion between his sisters, and Papiria was able to return to her former home –

where she lived out her final days in a state of reasonable security.

Cornelia Scipio, the older girl, married a cousin, once removed: Publius Scipio Nasio Corculum, whose father was a consul in 190. The two of them had several children, including Publius Scipio Nasica Serapio, who married Caecillia Metella; Publius Scipio Nasica, who married Licinia Crassa, and had a daughter Prima. Cornelia and Nasio also had Cornelia Scipionis, a daughter who married Cornelius Publius Lentulus.

If, looking at this family tree you are thinking, "Lot of marrying of cousins here," you would be right. The customs were different then, and the results of inbreeding not so very well known. In addition, these youngsters probably had a limited number of people from whom they were allowed to select a spouse – or their spouse might have been selected for them. Arranged marriages were not unusual for the times.

Scipio's youngest daughter, Cornelia Africana Minor, married Tiberius Sempronius Gracchus. They had twelve children, only three of whom lived to maturity: Tiberius Sempronius Gracchus, Gaius Sempronius Gracchus, and Sempronia, the only surviving daughter.

Tiberius Gracchi was killed by a "senatorial mob." Tiberius was often opposed to the Scipio line's point of view. He was somewhat conservative, and had begun to notice that there were problems at home. He advocated a return to the practice of dividing up newly conquered land among those who were without lands, while binding those men to existing estates – as had been the practice in earlier times in the empire. However, his suggestion was voted down in the senate – repeatedly. At that time, the lands were being divided among already landed houses, creating a situation where those who had power continued to accrue rather than raising up new plebeians. Eventually, his insistence and his policies, and his approach to getting them passed so angered the senators, that he was beaten to death by the rest of the senate. It signaled the end of the Republic and ushered in an age of rule by murder, intrigue, and violence.

His younger brother, Gaius, who was nine years his junior defended his brother at every turn, investing himself in reforms of Roman law and custom. He fell into conflict with Publius Scipio the Younger, who was married to Sempronia. Scipio the Younger disliked his wife, describing her as ugly and barren. Apparently the dislike was mutual, as Sempronia and her mother were suspected of being responsible for Scipio the Younger's untimely death.

Only Scipio Aemillianus approached Scipio Africanus the Elder's ability as a military strategist and diplomat. His management of the final razing of Carthage was a masterpiece of military engineering – which seems to have been his forte.

As the family dwindled, they became increasingly conservative in their views and in their abilities, until at last they dropped out of public notice. Or perhaps the latter was more the case than the former. Given the attitudes developed by Scipio Africanus the Elder, and the possibility that the men who were dissatisfied with the wives chosen for them by their parents, it is entirely possible that their tendency toward innovation and independence lived on in decedents who did not carry the name.

Chapter 11: Speculation, Surmise and a Little Fantasy

As mentioned in chapter 9 and chapter 10, Publius Scipio Africanis was a bitter man when he withdrew to his country villa. There were rumors and speculation about the lives of some of his contemporaries. We have scrutinized some of the real history; now we shall build just a little upon rumor, speculation and surmise to create a fantasy of might-have-been.

Let us set the scene. The year is 183 BC. Lucius and Publius Scipio are under suspicion of misappropriating funds that were collected from Antiochus. It is unlikely that this event would not have had impact on Aemilia, or that is would not have disturbed her marital life. But she has been visited by a friend – a woman whose life has been uprooted to the very core: Papiria, wife of Lucius Aemilius Paulus Macedonicus.

"I've lost it all," Papiria sobs, "He's divorced me. I've lost my children, my home, I don't even have enough money put by to rent a room. Aemilia, I don't know what to do."

"Did he say why?" Aemilia asked, gently wiping the tears away from her friend's face.

Papiria sighed, choked back another sob, and smiled sadly, "He didn't say, but I can guess. After four children, I am no longer so young and attractive as I once was. Oh, Aem, I have no idea how I shall go on – how I shall live. I have no desire to sell myself."

"Nonsense," Aemilia said briskly, "While it is distasteful, you have many skills. My needle work is by no means as fine as yours, nor are my skills in the dairy nearly as good. I have need of a new table runner to go with the new goblets Scipio allowed me to purchase. I will advance you some coin. I believe that there is a modest house for hire near where my cook lives – we will ask her. I will spread the word, and soon you will have enough work to keep you."

As so it was that Papiria was able to remain an independent woman, even though she was reduced to straitened circumstance. Aemilia told Scipio of the incident, of course, and he encouraged her to continue to hire Papiria for needle work and such assistance as they could afford. He, himself, was under some constraint as he struggled with censure. Publius Scipio knew that he had not misappropriated any funds, and he did not think that his brother had done so either. There was a rumor that some of the money that had been collected had been siphoned off to throw a party for troops – but there was no evidence to show that it was so, or that the money that was used came from an inappropriate source.

Indeed, it was money, politics and living space that created a temporary rift between Publius and Aemilia. Late one afternoon, Publius came home. His face was red with wrath. "Pack!" he commanded. "I'll not spend one more day in this town. I've had enough. We are leaving the city, just as quickly as we can throw our possessions in containers and load them into a cart. "But Publius!" Aemilia cried, "Our friends . . ."

"I have no friends in this gods deserted city!" Publius declared. With that, he retired to the family still room, where he gloomily settled himself in a favorite chair while he drowned his sorrows in one of the cheaper wines stored there. He was in too bad a mood to indulge in something that was expensive that would taste good. He had upheld Rome all his life, and now She had turned against him. He had walked her streets as Aedile, had fought her wars, and had in every way been a model citizen and soldier. He did not weep. He was too angry for that.

Seeing how upset he was, Aemilia went to do his bidding. Servants scuttled this way and that, collecting packing boxes and crates, along with straw and other things that would be needed to cushion the breakables. It was during this time of turmoil that Blossom found Publius lounging in the deserted room – all of the other servants were busy elsewhere, and Aemilia had gone to the temple for the daily ritual – his tunic askew and his face flushed with wine. She knelt before him, and offered him words of comfort. Before they knew it, she was offering him a more substantial sort of comfort than words. In the days that followed, it became almost a custom. Blossom would find an excuse not to attend the daily pilgrimage to the houses of the gods, and would worship in a most substantial way the one true god of her childhood – she had always liked and admired Publius, although Lucius sometimes teased in ways that were unkind.

However, before a fortnight had passed their belongings were loaded into wagons and they were on their way to their country villa. The brief affair between Blossom and Scipio ended for simple lack of opportunity.

Before they left the city, however, Aemilia found time to visit briefly with Papiria. "I'll be fine," Papiria said. "You've sent enough trade my way that I can manage – even though I am losing my best customer. But take my advice: if your husband looks to another for his pleasure, pretend you know nothing about it. This world is not made for women to be able to easily earn their own bread."

"Thank you for your advice," Aemilia said, "But I know my husband, and I am sure that he would never do that to me."

"You think you know him," Papiria sniffed delicately, "But men can surprise you – even the best of them – and not always in a good way. It is better to endure the situation in many cases rather than find yourself in such straitened circumstances as I now find myself."

Aemilia watched her friend leave, then returned to her packing. Publius arrived just in time to give the rooms a last check and to place a small casket behind the seat of the lead wagon. She then took her place in the seat behind the driver, and Publius rode alongside the lead wagon on his fine horse. The movement of the beast seemed to give him no pleasure, however, for he scowled at the road ahead. There were no flowers or well-wishers for this parade – only a few curious looks from passers-by.

Soon Aemilia realized that they were not going to the Scipio family farm. The miles passed by slowly, and at length they stopped at a small inn for the night. Most of the party made camp outside, while Aemilia had a room in the inn. Publius stayed with her for a while, but soon went back out to check the camp and their household. Perhaps he slipped into a certain tent or room and took some comfort there, or perhaps he protected his childhood friend by keeping a respectful distance in those times when he would not have been able to keep their meetings secret.

This set the pattern for the first three or four days. Then they moved beyond the areas where they could count on there being an inn. Publius unpacked his red war tent for the Aemilia and himself – it was his, after all. In some ways, it was more comfortable than the inns. For one thing, there were no bedbugs or fleas. For another, the linens were their own and had been laundered under the scrutiny of a slave who found it her business to make sure they were fresh.

As they continued southward, the air at night would swarm with mosquitos. The servants hung drapes of gauzy linen from Egypt around their beds to keep the humming insects away. Even so, the members of the party with fair skins woke each morning with welts from bites from the creatures.

It was almost a relief when they again began to come to small villages along the way. Publius explained to her that they were now in Compania, and would soon come to Liturnum, where he had purchased a small farm.

"But it is so far away from everything," Aemilia protested.

"We will not be far from Pompeii," Publius replied. "It is a bustling port town, so I am sure that we will find everything we need there. I know we have left your friends behind," he said gently, "but I am sure you will make new ones here."

Aemilia was quiet, remembering Papiria's words. How could she explain to her husband that while new friends were nice, they were not her old friends – the ones she might never see again.

Publius was different from the way he had been before the upsetting times with the Senate. Sometimes she hardly knew him. He seemed colder, more distant – and he had never been a demonstrative man. But in times past, he would joke or tell stories for her amusement. Now, all of that seemed to have departed. Often, he was somber or looked angry although he never raised either his hand or his voice to her.

When they reached their new villa, she found it to be a far cry from their comfortable town house. The rooms, including the solar were smaller; the bath was dank and cold, and frequently infested with crickets in addition to the ever-present mosquitos. Aemilia felt tired and listless. Scipio Africanus the younger, their oldest son, was frequently ill. Even with the help of her experienced staff, Aemilia felt the added work of living in the country. They did their own laundry, baked their own bread; there were no shops to send out to for a bit of something special or different.

Publius worked in the fields all day, and was moody and silent at table at night. Aemilia didn't notice at first, then she put it down to his being dissatisfied with her and with Rome. She was unhappy, lonely and miserable.

One day she noticed that Blossom, a serving maid – a slave, who had been inherited from the Scipio family estate, was moving more carefully than was usual. Blossom was a beautiful woman, lithe and strong. But on that particularly day she looked pale and sick. It took only a few minutes to learn that Blossom was in the family way, and only a few more sharp questions to discover that Publius was the father. The whole story came out – the days when Blossom had pleaded a headache to be excused from the daily rituals, the stillroom, and more recently since the move, the dairy.

"He is the master," Blossom said. "And he seemed so distraught. How could I refuse him? Oh, please, mistress, don't make me expose my baby – let me keep it."

"It will be from Publius, I'll not make you do that," Aemilia said, thinking furiously. She was angry – angry with Publius, angry with the woman for not telling her after the first time. But her own travails had been difficult, and she loved all four of her children, and it was likely she would have no more. She would not squander even one so misbegotten that came from Publius' seed. Furthermore, she thought, it could possible that she should be grateful to Blossom. Publius was certainly changed from the brash, boasting, supremely confident young man she had married. It could even be that she owed Blossom his life and sanity after the way the Senators had treated Publius.

She sighed. Were she to adopt the child, it would cause talk. There would be talk, and probably already had been. But she could organize security for mother and child.

"The smith is unwed," she commented. "Would you find him objectionable?"

"Not objectionable, mistress, but it is well known that he prefers boys to women. I doubt . . ."

"He will lack an heir, then. I think we can make this right. You will not lose your place here, the smith will gain a housekeeper and an heir. You will be secure, and so will your child." Aemilia immediately sent for the smith.

Blossom twisted the folds of the apron nervously in her hands. "The master . . . you'll not be angry with him?"

Aemilia gave a short bark of laughter. "Of course I'm angry with him. But fear not, he'll take no harm from me. Even this cheerless place is better than should be my lot if I divorced him." She thought of Papiria, living in one tiny room, scraping out a living by taking in fine sewing. Then her face softened, "More than that, Blossom, I am fond of him. We were wed at the direction of our fathers, but he is usually a kind man and a wise one. I'd be a poor wife to begrudge him such comfort as he has been able to find in your arms – and I'll be grateful that he looked no farther afield than our own household. But it must come to a stop. I am sorry that you will pay the price for this, but I am afraid that I do not intend to share my husband. So...no slipping out and cheating on the smith – even if he has his own amusements."

Aemilia and Publius were closeted in their private rooms for a long time that afternoon, but they emerged arm in arm in time to attend the wedding of Blossom to the local smith. If

Blossom's first and only child was birthed a little earlier than was seemly, it was not an unusual thing for first babies. If she and the smith seemed more like friends and business partners than husband and wife, that was not unusual enough to excite comment.

Amazingly enough, after that the Scipio home became more cheerful. Writers, generals and other famous people came to visit from time to time. Fires burned on the formerly cold hearths, and the master and mistress were often seen strolling around the fields together or sitting with their heads over lists of items and numbers. The mistress learned about preserving foods, just as she had once learned where to find the best shops for bargains in order to stretch the family resources.

Peace was restored, but it was soon clear that Publius was truly not a well man. His breath came short, and sometimes his chest pained him. He took to drinking mulled wine with herbs in it of an evening in an effort to still the pains. One evening, when the pain was worse than usual, and his bones ached in ways they had never ached on the battlefield he spoke with Aemilia, the Grammaticus – his old teacher, who was now a freedman who managed the farms accounts, and his friend, Laelius. "Don't take my body back to Rome," he said.

Aemilia made a sound, but he put his hand on hers, and said, "Hush now, I know what this body is telling me. I have been too ill, too long of late. I have put it to hard usage, now I must pay the cost." He clasped her fingers tenderly for a moment. "But I'll not give my bones back to the city that spurned my final efforts and tried to accuse my brother and I of treason. Lucius did not steal those 500 talents, and although I think I know who did, I honestly cannot dispute the use to which they were put. I fought long with men who were loyal because they felt the cause for which they fought was just – and they did it on short rations, and minimal gear. They had back pay owed; I'll not mourn that the money they helped earn went to their pleasure."

"But I'll not have my final resting place be in a city that has forgotten honor, forgotten the men that fight for her. Let my bones lie here, where my labor has been honest and the returns – although often small – are won through the skills of my household. Don't worry, Aemilia, you are provided for and so are the children – although they could scarcely be called children now." Laelius related this conversation to a famed writer of the time at a later date.

Although that week had been one of debilitating illness for Publius, he was up and around soon after. But his prediction was not wrong. He had used his body hard during the years in Spain, and he had never been as robust as his brother. At length, he died, and was buried quietly, attended by his widow, his one-time lover, his children and the other members of his household.

And if, in that far-away place, a certain blacksmith's son looked nothing like his legal father, and if he had a knack for making things work, for creating plans, then one could say that the seed did not fall on stony ground and that the genius of the Cornelius line lived on – even if the name dwindled away.

Of course, this tale is almost pure fiction. It is based on a few chance lines in other accounts and is fabricated from likelihood. Given the nature of the stories recorded in mythology, we could have ascribed a completely different response to Aemilia. No one knows the name of the household woman who was the recipient of Scipio's attentions, or whether she was willing or not. Slaves and servants alike had little choice in those days. In keeping with the evidence given that Aemilia engaged in daily rituals, that she loved her fine clothes and ritual vessels, I have extrapolated that she would have preferred to quietly find a way to deal with the fallout. As for implying that the blacksmith was not one for women, men who preferred boys or other men were well known in that region.

There are references to the possibility that Scipio did stray from his marriage bed – even if he did return the chieftain's daughter to her parents and to her betrothed, without touching her. Soldiers did, in those days, often avail themselves of the camp followers. It is written in some accounts that Hannibal had a lover in Spain, and that he fathered a son. But no further mention is made of either the woman or the child in any of the accounts. Possibly, that was because after Hannibal made his trip over the Alps, he never returned to Spain and no arrangements had been made for the woman or the child to follow him into Rome or back to Carthage.

As has been mentioned, one of the big differences between Scipio and Hannibal was Scipio's easy way with words and his ability to make friends. Even toward the end, when Scipio had turned away from Rome, he was visited by friends at his farm in Liturnum. Hannibal, on the other hand, allowed only his brothers to get close to him. He was a soldier's soldier, working long hours into the night, inspiring loyalty from his troops by his actions rather than by harsh rules or punishments.

After his trip over the Alps, Hannibal fell ill. One of his eyes became infected – an account that mentioned this suggested that he might have had conjunctivas, that common school room malady sometimes referred to as "pink eye." In the field, in a setting that did not encourage or provide opportunity for personal care, it is not impossible that such an illness could become severe. On the rare occasions when the commander cold sleep, his men took great care not to disturb him. This speaks of a man who inspired loyalty beyond that garnered through a mercenary's pay.

In many ways, Hannibal and Scipio are an interesting study in contrasts. Scipio was the son of a patrician household – even though it seems likely that they were richer in reputation than in cash. Hannibal Barca was in the field with his father Hamilcar by the age of ten. It could be said that he learned how to wage war at his father's knee and he gave little care to honor or honorability. His affections were primarily reserved for his brothers and uncles who were also doing their best to take over Iberia, or Spain as it would later be known. Hannibal was the elder by nearly ten years, and it was the records of his battles that served as Scipio's instruction in the school of espionage and dirty deeds, as it were. Scipio also proved to be Hannibal's greatest challenge. Whereas the other Roman generals adhered to the same old formations and methods, Scipio observed how Hannibal was able to use smart tactics, even dishonorable tactics, to win encounters. He could certainly see how Hannibal had managed to survive for twelve years in the Italian peninsula with minimal support from Carthage. Scipio copied those tactics, turning them against Hannibal, and adding his own version of dirty deeds for good measure.

Both were able commanders, and both were betrayed by their home city. Whereas Scipio was able to settle down in the country and run an estate, however, Hannibal was forced to run to other courts. Winding up in Antiochus III's court did little to assist him, however. His military genius was worth very little when he was given undisciplined men who were unaccustomed to precision moves. In the end, Antiochus was prepared to give him up to the Romans. Hannibal took poison rather than end up in the hands of the Romans.

Would that actually have been such a terrible fate? Or did Hannibal, like Scipio, have a body that was worn out with years in the field, eating bad food, sleeping in discomfort and always, always on the move lest an enemy catch up with you. Carthage had a very direct way of dealing with those perceived as failures. Perhaps he expected similar treatment from the Romans, and was taking steps to deal with it ahead of time. Perhaps his loyalty was such that he had secrets that he preferred to take to the grave. Or perhaps he was already dying, and the poison only shortened the time before his death.

Whatever the reason, the result was that these two able commanders died within two years of each other. It was something of the closing of an era.

Rome would go on to become an empire. Carthage would rise from the ignominy of the Second Punic war to once again become a bustling trading nation, but would be struck down by Scipio Aemilius and laid waste in the Third Punic War. Much of that would be because Rome had developed an obsession with Carthage and the Big Bad Enemy that must be destroyed. There were senators who called for it daily in the senate and promoted the idea that Carthage was a Bad Seed that should not be allowed to grow.

Some accounts of the destruction of Carthage say that the land was salted so that nothing would grow there. Other historians say that the salting was a later embellishment and that it never happened. However, the location was ritually cursed. The substance of the curse was that nothing would again grow there – neither crops or buildings. This proved to be a bit of a problem when Rome wanted to build its own city on that spot. The Romans were, in many ways, a superstitious lot. A curse would have had real meaning to them. Perhaps that should be a lesson to subsequent generations – be careful of the legends you create because they can become a weapon that will turn in your hand and bite you. One of the old legends of the region is the story of the dragon's teeth, which when sown in a plowed field would become an invincible army. The method for defeating them was to throw a rock at one, convince the guy next to him that he was being attacked, and then stand back and watch them battle it out amongst themselves until they were all slain.

One has to wonder about some things. The area around the Mediterranean has been the scene of so many epic historical battles, it is almost as if someone had sown the whole region with dragons teeth, then thrown the rock and stood back. Perhaps this is a skewed perception, an incorrect historical view. But it does cause one to speculate as to why that particular region is constantly contended. Some of it is location, some of it is resources. But perhaps some of it has to do with the temperament of the people who live there. This is only speculation. Or perhaps someone goes through that region nightly, sowing dragons teeth.

Chapter 12: Some Thoughts on Written Records

Tracing the lives of the rich and famous centuries later presents a variety of challenges. As has been previously mentioned, Scipio Publius Africanis is a classic case. On the one hand, he is sufficiently famous as a military genius that accounts of his battles have survived as military lore, or even legend.

The problem with this is that military legends – even ones that are carefully crafted and recorded – tend to be like fisherman's stories. The numbers get a little exaggerated, episodes get blown up larger than life, various accounts fail to match. In fact, in some cases, historians can even begin to doubt that an event truly happened. The Fall of Troy is a good example of this syndrome.

The Battle of Zama is an example of an event which is well-recorded, but is doubted in some circles. As discussed in an earlier chapter, historians note that we aren't sure of the exact location of the battle. Archeologists have not found evidence of a battle on Zama plain.

Yet this battle is one that has a plethora of records about it. Was it a propaganda event manufactured by Rome to counterbalance Cannae? Was it an ordinary maneuver blown up into epic proportions? Did it actually occur? Some account question the veracity of the records, contending that it was a hoax intended to make Rome looks good. It is well known, after all, that the victors write history. It is only later generations that look through the records, trying to ascertain the veracity of the accounts in order to develop a better idea of what actually occurred. A desire to look great, to sway the home population to see an event as essential for national security, and to dissuade enemies from thinking that a nation is a soft target. That last can be an important point for deterring unnecessary or unwanted wars.

Accounts of personal events – how Publius and Aemilia met, whether or not he was faithful, how she felt about the move to Compania – are even more hazy. Chapter 11 is built entirely on one or two sentences of an account that mentions that Publius might have had an affair, and that Aemilia, not wishing to share Papiria's fate, chose to publicly ignore the incident. I have made my fictional Aemilia a little warmer and more understanding than perhaps is likely. Aemilia was fond of her public displays of devotion to the gods, her fine retinue and her fine ritual vessels. It is unlikely that she happily acquiesced to moving out of the city onto a farm.

It is known that Publius was angry with Rome over the lawsuits and accusations that marred Lucius's triumphant return from Asia. He was also tired of the vacillations of the Senate and the mercurial shifting of the popular vote of the people. Of this much we can be fairly sure. It is mentioned by both Livy and Polybius, and it makes sense. But many of the things that we would really like to know, such as Publius date of birth, the exact birth order of he and his sibling, and whether or not he was really born of a Cesarean – or whether that was simply propaganda, is lost in the sifting sands of time. Was his mother still alive when he proclaimed to the world that she had been unfaithful to his father with a god? Or was that a subtle reflection of a real event? In all probability, that particular claim falls under the same heading as some of the tall tales about Daniel Boone and Davy Crockett, when they are out claiming relationships with wild creatures an their ability to whip alligators and wild cats. Publius Scipio Africanus was, after all, reputed to be a golden-tongued orator, capable of swaying crowds, influencing hardened military veterans – and doubtless persuading virgins to his bed if he should so desire. His was, in his day, the hero of the hour, the quick fix for unsolvable problems and even the blazing sword of revenge. Small wonder that the quieter side of his life should have been obscured by lack of attention or accounts smudged by bombastic prevarication.

Battles, on the other hand, are covered in loving and precise detail by a variety of different sources. Apparently, these events were the things that the Romans found important. Social sentiment was reserved for graphitti and gravestones. Perhaps that reflects something of the Roman mind. Even their legends and stories tend to focus on the combative side of things. Can we say that our modern tales are so very different? A few hours viewing of that modern orator, broadcast media, brings to the viewer explosions, combat, plots, vengeance, and more. Only a scant few minutes of an episode or cinematic story are devoted to ordinary events or even to more tender relationships. Perhaps this says something more about the human race in general than it does about the Romans specifically.

According to some accounts, there were other historical records. Publius is said to have kept a journal – but that is long lost. It is said that there was a chapter in Plutarch's lives about him, but that is also lost. The ages are not kind to written material – not even that which is engraved in stone or marked on clay tablets. Papyrus, sheep skin parchment, and other organic matter is subject to decay and to burning. Generations of editing the past by flame, destruction of libraries by zealots, and simply the ravages of time tend to obscure the past.

This makes these histories fertile ground for fictionalizing. Unlike the Adamses, who were the first political family in the United States to have filled the presidency twice with different members, very little that is personal remains of this famous Roman general.

Even going back and reading translations of the primary sources is of little assistance. The historians of the time fill in their pages with ranting at the gods or long flowery speeches to other political figures. It should be equally noted that while historical figures such as Cleopatra or Helen of Troy are credited with a degree of influence, they are mentioned more in passing than in any other way. Gods and Goddesses figure large in speeches that the heroes are supposed to have made. One suspects that this speaks more to the tastes of the theatre audiences of the day having loved a good spectacle than to veracity. In any case, home life and family are given short shrift in the annals that record the deeds of Publius Scipio Cornelius Africanus the Elder.

Again, we can look to other accounts to gain some idea of how people behaved in those days. We can, again, look at the climate, and real distances between locations and how it might have been to move a household. We can look at statues, paintings and mosaics to discover how people dressed. We can even turn to regulations, which dictated what was worn by each class – particularly for the men. Human emotions are pretty consistent, even if human customs change. Some people are tolerant, some are not. Fear, affection, sorrow, and anger hold true across the board as responses that a person might have. Child mortality might have led to customs such as not naming a child until after his or her first birthday, but parental affection for a child usually still existed, and most frequently begins with first contact with a warm, wiggling baby body. As in many societies, boy children were valued more than girls in ancient Rome – an odd state of affairs, biologically speaking. But humans are the animals that rationalize – rather than being rational.

So what can we gain from these histories? Perhaps, as Shakespeare wrote, "The good that men do is oft interred with their bones," right along with their personal histories, the very real things that they felt and thought, their fears, challenges and anxieties. Writing was not a universal skill, although the Romans were not an illiterate society. Classes were held in the open square of a city, and the boys taught there were disciplined with a rod. Girls, if they were fortunate enough to be taught to read, write and figure, were taught at home. However, learning was a privilege ofte reserved for the upper class and for scribes and priests. It was used to record tithes, taxes, and numbers of soldiers. Small wonder that the primary places we find the emotional responses of individuals are tombstones and on the walls of their houses.

Looking at the coins that remain displaying the balding head of Publius Scipio Africanus, he was a man of strong feelings off the battlefield as well as on. But his deepest feelings, or the things that he felt sufficiently important to record in a journal, are lost to us. We don't even know what sort of medium he used as the pages in his journal. Was it papyrus from Egypt? Was it parchment? We can be certain that its leaves were not clay, for clay tablets would have been too difficult to carry in a soldier's kit. The deeds of Publius the soldier and commander remain for us to read and speculate over; the thoughts and feelings of Publius the man are more difficult to obtain. Even after cross-referencing many sources, including accounts of his supposed rants to the gods, although his military might is plainly displayed, getting a handle on the man himself – his feelings, his ideas, his dreams and aspirations – is much more difficult.

Therefore, we extrapolate, we fictionalize, and we fantasize. Who was this man who defeated one of the most creative and able commanders of his day? Who was this man who was sufficiently canny to study the moves of his opponent? Like two great chess players using live playing pieces, Hannibal and Scipio's war spanned nearly twenty years of conflict. These two great generals studied each other's tactics. They spied upon each other, they each tried to out-guess their opponent.

More than that, it was the opening for the third Punic war. In fact, one of Scipio's grandson was instrumental in the final demise of Carthage.

It seems that in addition to being an able strategist, like his grandfather, Scipio Aemilius, who also earned the title Africanus, was a talented engineer. With that in mind, one must then consider the influence these two generals, these fighting men, had upon their world and the world that was to follow. Indeed, we can still see conflict in the areas where they once battled. If we could resolve their wars, would we be able to resolve our own?

Who can say? Perhaps our children or our children's children will look over this account or similar ones, shake their heads and say, "Why did they choose to record these things? Why did they not tell us more about that?" They might even say, "Why was so much of it electronically recorded? Why was so much of it on impermanent materials such as paper? The only things we have left are words chiseled on monuments." Or will digital media become more permanent, and will they instead shake their heads over the multitudinous accounts of cute kittens, crazy pratfalls and semi-spontaneous instances of flash dance and ask, "Why didn't someone show us how to extrude wire? Or plant vegetables? Where are the plans for various field tactics? Why can't we find those?"

We who can speak with friends or family who are half the world away, and have access to news, books and documents of all sorts, are, in some ways, no better informed than many of the plebeians who lived in Rome. We read for pleasure, we read to learn about the latest Hollywood or Bollywood scandal, but we avoid dealing with the more serious topics in our world. Perhaps that is a natural thing. Goodness knows, it those weren't serious messages that were scratched on the outsides of the houses in Pompeii. Even some of the messages inscribed on tombstones show a sense of humor or the foibles of humanity. It is only the scholars, such as Plutarch, Polybius or Livy who has worked their way through serious accounts of the various battles that occurred so long ago.

The records that we find left by the common people, through such media as the well-preserved ruins at Pompeii indicate that the Roman people were probably not so greatly different from us. Most of them were concerned with the ordinary day to day details of their lives. They were focused on their sweethearts or their business rivals. Were Scipio and Hannibal greatly different? Or were their concerns simply a little larger than those around them? The scholars leave us little to go on in this regard. They were more concerned with the major political issues of the day than they were with such things as birthdates, wedding dates, or whether the great commander of a particular army preferred beef or pork. Yet it is these small things that flesh out the character of a historical figure. Lacking such information, we must become as the novelist or playwright, ascribing motivation to certain actions as we peer darkly through the telescope of time into a world that could have had completely different motivations from the ones that govern our world today.

Perhaps that is the answer. Perhaps we should look at the things that these ancients emphasized, the things that they recorded, as a means of understanding the things that they valued: prowess in battle, excellent oration, integrity in the face of difficulty, and the ability to leave wife and child behind and go make a barrier against the enemy using only their bodies, a shield made of wood and hide, and such weapons as could be held in their hands. Could it be that this is the message that these elders from a past and a culture that is long ago would truly wish for us to understand? We can but speculate and wonder.

Afterword

Some say that the passing of Publius Scipio Cornelius Africanus marked the beginning of the great age of the Roman Empire. Or perhaps it only marked a different sort of beginning. History is more like a great stream that runs in a circle rather than a river that has a head water and a delta where it exits into the sea. Perhaps it is even more accurate to say that reasoning by analogy is flawed and presents only single way to provide understanding to those who are not familiar with an event or process.

Certainly, Publius saw the beginnings of the Third Punic War. His adoptive grandson, Scipio Aemillius Africanus the younger, fostered and cared for by his oldest son, the augur, was a central figure in the third Punic war and the actions that finished Carthage for good and all.

Readers might recall that at the end of the Second Punic War, Carthage had been forbidden to declare war on any other nation without permission from Rome. Numidia, having become something of an ally of Rome under Masinissa, grew increasingly aggressive toward Carthage, attacking and taking over small towns and lands that had traditionally belonged to Carthage. At last, Carthage had had enough. They retaliated to an attack, thus tacitly declaring war on Numidia.

This action was all the excuse that Rome needed to come down hard on their erstwhile enemy. Hannibal, who had proved to be an able governor had fled the city when her nobility had grown restive under his policy of tightening belts rather than imposing more taxes in order to balance budgets. Perhaps it was after his governing hand was removed that Numidia grew bold, and the aristocrats irritated that Rome was handed this ready-made excuse to come down hard on their former enemy.

Rome sent notice to Carthage that because of its violation of treaty, that they intended to raze the city, and burn it to the ground. Carthage did not respond as directed –

which was to move 16 kilometers inland and rebuild. Instead, they released all their slaves, and began to prepare for battle.

Carthage had amazing defenses. They had 34 kilometers of defensive wall – in triple layers in some areas. The harbor was also well defended. The initial attack on the city, led by Manius Manilius and Marcius Censorinus did not go well. For one thing, they were unable to successfully block the harbor, and Carthage continued to receive supplies by sea. For another, in the hot summer of 148 BC, the besiegers were hit by a plague.

The city of Utica had defected to Rome, but Hippacra, another city, remained stubborn in its defense of Carthage, successfully resisting the forces led by Consul Piso. The Numidians were under a new king, Bithyas, and had also swapped sides as it were – sending 800 cavalry to swell the defense of Hippacra. Things did not look good for Rome.

Then a new player came on the scene. You will recall that Publius Scipio, son of Scipio Africanus, was unable to serve Rome due to health problems; but that apparently did not deter his ability to train up a new Scipio – his adopted son Scipio Amelius. This young Scipio was like his grandfather in ability. He not only had studied the maneuvers made by his grandfather and by Hannibal, he had a knack for engineering.

Under his guidance, the Romans built a better siege wall around Carthage – one that enabled them to attack the Carthaginian defenses. He also built a siege mole – a contraption similar to a tower, that contained a catapult of sorts. This mole prevented ships from being able to sail into the harbor without running the risk of being holed by one of the projectiles from the tower. With their supplies cut off, the Carthaginians were in a desperate way.

Meanwhile, the rest of the Carthaginian army is being held at Nepheris. With a firm chokehold on the harbor, Scipio Amelius felt sufficiently confident to send forces to help deal with it.

In the spring of 146, using the mole, the Romans force their way into the harbor. Then begins the hand to hand fighting in the streets, with the Romans forcing the defenders back and back through the streets and the Carthaginians resisting with all of their strength.

Commander Hasdrubal and 900 Roman deserters resisted nearly to the last in the central citadel. He gave himself up, but his wife threw herself and her two children onto the funeral pyre for the Carthaginian fighters. Such was the depth of her shame and outrage that he should have surrendered.

The city burned for seventeen days. A population of over 150,000 had been reduced to less than 50,000. The land where Carthage stood was ritually cursed so that no one would rebuild on that location.

The Punic culture, however, did not disappear, but continued in small villages in the countryside. It was not until the reign of Julius Caesar that Carthage would be rebuilt.

Publius Scipio's descendants would be part of the continued saga of the Roman Empire, with its dramas, its betrayals, its alliances and foreign wars. But it was almost as if with the destruction of Carthage, so also began the slow downfall of Rome.

It was a slow process – a slave uprising in Rome, a defection of allies, a marriage between a Roman Emperor and an Egyptian princess, complicated with the princess having an affair with a Roman senator. The leader of a new religion is born, stirring up the Hebrews, and the Druids revolted in Great Britain. Steadily, inexorably, the world changed.

Or is that merely a perception? Perhaps the more the world changes, the more it stays the same. Therein lies the real value of studying history. When we read of the wild emotions of these long-ago people, they seem almost unreal. Wives who drink poison or throw themselves on funeral pyres? Ingesting poison carried about in a ring, as Hannibal was said to have done rather than be turned over to Rome?

Yet is that any more strange than a woman who has her ribs surgically removed so that she can resemble a cartoon character?

These are questions that perhaps will be answered by another generation – one that might find our customs, mores and responses just as strange as we might find those recorded about those old Romans or Carthaginians.

Bibliography

Scullard, Howard Hays.(20150 Scipio Africanus the Elder.
Encyclopedia Britannica, online.
https://www.britannica.com/biography/Scipio-Africanus-the-Elder

Scullard, Howard Hayes Publius Scipio Cornelius Africanus
(236-184/3 BC) Latin Library,
http://www.thelatinlibrary.com/imperialism/notes/scipio.html

Locri Epzephryii https://www.britannica.com/place/Locri-Epizephyrii

Clare, John. (?) Livy on the Battle of Zama, 202 BC
http://www.johndclare.net/AncientHistory/Hannibal_Sources8.html

Polybius, Histories.
http://www.perseus.tufts.edu/hopper/text?doc=Perseus%3Atext%3A1999.01.0234%3Abook%3D15%3Achapter%3D12

Calabria https://en.wikipedia.org/wiki/Calabria

Locris https://en.wikipedia.org/wiki/Locris

Augur https://en.wikipedia.org/wiki/Augur

Publius Cornelius Scipio Nasica Corculu

https://en.wikipedia.org/wiki/Publius_Cornelius_
Scipio_Nasica_Corculum

Scipio Africanus
https://en.wikipedia.org/wiki/Scipio_Africanus

Publius Cornelius Scipio Africanus

https://www.geni.com/people/Publius-Cornelius-
Scipio-Africanus/6000000005944438076

Mark, Joshua J. Scipio Africanus the Elder, Ancient History

http://www.ancient.eu/Scipio_Africanus_the_Eld
er/

Publius Cornelius Scipio Africanus (236 – 184/3 B.C.)

http://www.thelatinlibrary.com/imperialism/note
s/scipio.html

Carthage, Roman Empire http://www.roman-
empire.net/republic/carthage.html

Battle of Zama http://www.unrv.com/empire/battle-of-
zama.php

Mark, Joshua J. *Hannibal, Ancient History*
http://www.ancient.eu/hannibal/

Hannibal http://www.biography.com/people/hannibal-9327767

Tiberius Semphronius Gracchus, Biography, Encyclopedia
    Brittanica
    https://www.britannica.com/biography/Tiberius-Sempronius-Gracchus#ref87735

http://sites.psu.edu/cams101groupi2014/carthage/siege-of-saguntum/

ex.oup.com/view/10.1093/oi/authority.20110803095639
    712

Battle of Ilipa http://www.roman-empire.net/army/ilipa.html

Trebia and Trasimere
    https://sites.psu.edu/hannibal/battles-of-trebia-and-trasimene/

Siege of Tyre Map (Examples of Siege Moles)

http://sillysoft.net/lux/maps/SIEGE%20OF%20TYRE

Third Punic War

http://www.ancient.eu/Third_Punic_War/

Roman Time Line

http://courses.wcupa.edu/jones/his101/web/t-roman.htm

The Punic Wars

http://www.historyworld.net/wrldhis/plaintexthistories.asp?historyid=ac53

The Punic Wars: The History of the Conflict that Destroyed Carthage and Made Rome A Global Power, by Charles River Editors. July 13, 2015

Manufactured by Amazon.ca
Bolton, ON